NEW DIRECTIONS FOR
A Publication of the Am

William R. Shadish, *University of Memphis*
EDITOR-IN-CHIEF

Guiding Principles for Evaluators

William R. Shadish
University of Memphis

Dianna L. Newman
University at Albany/SUNY

Mary Ann Scheirer
Program Evaluation Consultant

Christopher Wye
National Academy of Public Administration

EDITORS

Number 66, Summer 1995

JOSSEY-BASS PUBLISHERS
San Francisco

GUIDING PRINCIPLES FOR EVALUATORS
William R. Shadish, Dianna L. Newman, Mary Ann Scheirer, Christopher Wye (eds.)
New Directions for Program Evaluation, no. 66
William R. Shadish, Editor-in-Chief

© 1995 by Jossey-Bass Inc., Publishers. All rights reserved.

No part of this issue may be reproduced in any form—except for a brief quotation (not to exceed 500 words) in a review or professional work—without permission in writing from the publishers.

Microfilm copies of issues and articles are available in 16mm and 35mm, as well as microfiche in 105mm, through University Microfilms Inc., 300 North Zeeb Road, Ann Arbor, Michigan 48106-1346.

LC 85-644749   ISSN 0164-7989   ISBN 0-7879-9924-5

NEW DIRECTIONS FOR PROGRAM EVALUATION is part of The Jossey-Bass Education Series and is published quarterly by Jossey-Bass Inc., Publishers, 350 Sansome Street, San Francisco, California 94104-1342.

Subscriptions for 1995 cost $56.00 for individuals and $78.00 for institutions, agencies, and libraries.

EDITORIAL CORRESPONDENCE should be sent to the Editor-in-Chief, William R. Shadish, Department of Psychology, University of Memphis, Memphis, Tennessee 38152.

Manufactured in the United States of America. Nearly all Jossey-Bass books, jackets, and periodicals are printed on recycled paper that contains at least 50 percent recycled waste, including 10 percent postconsumer waste. Many of our materials are also printed with vegetable-based inks; during the printing process, these inks emit fewer volatile organic compounds (VOCs) than petroleum-based inks. VOCs contribute to the formation of smog.

NEW DIRECTIONS FOR PROGRAM EVALUATION
Sponsored by the American Evaluation Association
(A Joint Organization of the Evaluation Research Society and the Evaluation Network)

EDITOR-IN-CHIEF

William R. Shadish   University of Memphis

EDITORIAL ADVISORY BOARD

Betsy Jane Becker	Michigan State University
Richard A. Berk	University of California, Los Angeles
Leonard Bickman	Vanderbilt University
Howard S. Bloom	New York University
Robert F. Boruch	University of Pennsylvania
Donald T. Campbell	Lehigh University
Thomas C. Chalmers	Harvard University School of Public Health
Eleanor Chelimsky	U.S. General Accounting Office
Huey-tsyh Chen	University of Akron
Thomas D. Cook	Northwestern University
David S. Cordray	Vanderbilt University
James Earl Davis	University of Delaware
David M. Fetterman	Stanford University
James Joseph Heckman	University of Chicago
Larry V. Hedges	University of Chicago
John G. Heilman	Auburn University
Michael Hendricks	MH Associates
Karen C. Holden	University of Wisconsin, Madison
V. Joseph Holz	University of Chicago
Ernest R. House	University of Colorado
Dionne J. Jones	National Urban League
Henry M. Levin	Stanford University
Laura C. Leviton	University of Pittsburgh
Richard J. Light	Harvard University
Mark W. Lipsey	Claremont Graduate School
Anna-Marie Madison	University of North Texas
Melvin M. Mark	The Pennsylvania State University
Georg E. Matt	San Diego State University
Richard McCleary	University of California, Irvine
Richard Nathan	State University of New York, Albany
Michael Quinn Patton	Union Institute Graduate School
Emil J. Posavac	Loyola University of Chicago
Steve W. Raudenbush	Michigan State University
Charles S. Reichardt	University of Denver
David Rindskopf	CUNY Graduate Center
Peter H. Rossi	University of Massachusetts
Henry S. Sacks	Mount Sinai School of Medicine
Leonard Saxe	Brandeis University
Michael Scriven	The Evaluation Center, Western Michigan University
Lee Sechrest	University of Arizona
Nick L. Smith	Syracuse University
Richard C. Sonnichsen	Federal Bureau of Investigation, Washington, D.C.
Robert Stake	University of Illinois
William M. K. Trochim	Cornell University
Michael J. Wargo	U.S. General Accounting Office
Carol H. Weiss	Harvard University
Steven G. West	Arizona State University
Joseph S. Wholey	University of Southern California
Aaron Wildavsky	University of California, Berkeley
J. Douglas Willms	University of British Columbia
Paul Wortman	State University of New York, Stony Brook
Christopher Wye	National Academy of Public Administration

AMERICAN EVALUATION ASSOCIATION, C/O RITA O'SULLIVAN, SCHOOL OF EDUCATION, UNIVERSITY OF NORTH CAROLINA AT GREENSBORO, GREENSBORO, NORTH CAROLINA 27412

Editorial Policy and Procedures

NEW DIRECTIONS FOR PROGRAM EVALUATION (NDPE), a quarterly sourcebook, is an official publication of the American Evaluation Association. NDPE publishes empirical, methodological, and theoretical works on all aspects of evaluation and related fields. Substantive areas may include any program, field, or issue with which evaluation is concerned, such as government performance, tax policy, energy, environment, mental health, education, job training, medicine, and public health. Also included are such topics as product evaluation, personnel evaluation, policy analysis, and technology assessment. In all cases, the focus on evaluation is more important than the substantive topics. We are particularly interested in encouraging a diversity of evaluation perspectives and experiences and in expanding the boundaries of our field beyond the evaluation of social programs.

NDPE does not consider or publish unsolicited single manuscripts. Each issue of NDPE is devoted to a single topic, with contributions solicited, organized, reviewed, and edited by a guest editor. Issues may take any of several forms, such as a series of related chapters, a debate, or a long article followed by brief critical commentaries. In all cases, the proposals must follow a specific format, which can be obtained from the editor-in-chief. These proposals are sent to members of the editorial board and to relevant substantive experts for peer review. The process may result in acceptance, a recommendation to revise and resubmit, or rejection. However, NDPE is committed to working constructively with potential guest editors to help them develop acceptable proposals.

Lois-ellin Datta, Editor-in-Chief
P.O. Box 383768
Waikoloa, HI 96738

Jennifer C. Greene, Associate Editor
Department of Human Service Studies
Cornell University
Ithaca, NY 14853-4401

Gary Henry, Associate Editor
Public Administration and Urban Studies
Georgia State University
Atlanta, GA 30302-4039

CONTENTS

EDITORS' NOTES 1
William R. Shadish, Dianna L. Newman, Mary Ann Scheirer, Christopher Wye

1. Developing the Guiding Principles 3
William R. Shadish, Dianna L. Newman, Mary Ann Scheirer, Christopher Wye
This chapter presents some history relevant to the American Evaluation Association *Guiding Principles for Evaluators*, the processes used to create them, and some of the issues considered and controversies examined in the process.

2. Guiding Principles for Evaluators 19
American Evaluation Association, Task Force on Guiding Principles for Evaluators
Presented here is the version of the American Evaluation Association *Guiding Principles for Evaluators* that was approved and copyrighted by the AEA board of directors and subsequently adopted by vote of the AEA membership.

3. Principled Evaluation: A Critique of the AEA Guiding Principles 27
Ernest R. House
The American Evaluation Association's succinct *Guiding Principles for Evaluators* quietly establish new boundaries for addressing ethical problems of the profession.

4. A Twenty-Year Veteran's Reflections on the *Guiding Principles for Evaluators* 35
Robert W. Covert
Comparing the American Evaluation Association Guiding Principles with other sets of evaluation standards, this chapter addresses reactions to the principles and concludes with recommendations for their use.

5. Standards and Principles 47
James R. Sanders
The American Evaluation Association Guiding Principles and the Joint Committee Program Evaluation Standards have stated intentions that sound alike, but are they? This analysis leads to the conclusion that they are different in important ways.

6. Comments on the Guiding Principles 53
Eleanor Chelimsky
As useful as they are, the American Evaluation Association Guiding Principles fail to appreciate the precarious position of the evaluator who speaks truth to power, and their near total focus on elaborating further responsibilities for the evaluator may increase the evaluator's vulnerability to partisan attack.

7. Doing Good and Getting It Right 55
Peter H. Rossi
Judging the American Evaluation Association principles to be weak statements, difficult to apply in concrete circumstances, and potentially misleading through ambiguity, the author argues for more concern with doing good research rather than getting everyone's approval.

8. Ethics and Internal Evaluators 61
Robert G. Lovell
Demand for program evaluation has led many government agencies to develop in-house evaluation units, and a web of possible conflicts of interest presents internal evaluators with decisions about ethical actions not encountered by an independent evaluator.

9. An Independent Consultant's Perspective on the Guiding 69
Principles
Tara D. Knott
This chapter addresses the concerns that full-time evaluators in private practice have about the uses and value of the American Evaluation Association Guiding Principles.

10. International Perspectives on the Guiding Principles 77
Michael Hendricks, Ross F. Conner
A response to the American Evaluation Association Guiding Principles from the perspective of evaluators working in settings outside the United States is presented here.

11. Identifying and Respecting Differences Among Participants 91
in Evaluation Studies
Donna M. Mertens
Drawing on literature from the field of ethics in research and on multicultural, feminist ethical principles, the author explores methodological implications for evaluation practice.

12. The Future of Ethics in Evaluation: Developing the Dialogue 99
Dianna L. Newman
The author presents an agenda of issues related to the future development of ethics in evaluation and suggests initial steps in addressing these issues, emphasizing the role of evaluators, clients, and organizations supporting evaluation.

INDEX 111

Editors' Notes

Professions are marked by a number of features rarely shared by academic specialties. One of these is a code of ethics or standards that professionals aspire to follow. Several perceived needs tend to give rise to such codes. The primary need is probably this: when professional practitioners have frequent and influential contact with clients on matters of import, those clients need to know how those interactions are likely to affect client well-being. Professional evaluation engenders such a need. Evaluators spend other peoples' money doing evaluation, often huge amounts of money. They do so frequently, in every state and major city in the nation. They do so for nearly every major agency in the public sector and for an increasingly large number of private sector organizations, in academic and nonacademic settings. They are asked to address questions that often bear on the most controversial and persistent policy questions of our time. They do all this in competition with other groups who want to either do the evaluation or do something else with the evaluation money. With all this at stake, evaluators, their clients, and all the other stakeholders to evaluation realize that they stand to benefit from greater clarity about what to expect from evaluation. Codes of professional conduct are one way to begin to clarify these expectations. The American Evaluation Association (AEA) board of directors had such matters in mind when it formed a task force to create the AEA *Guiding Principles for Evaluators*. The task force was created in November 1992 and disbanded just over one year later, in January 1994. In the span, the task force not only helped to develop a set of guiding principles for evaluators but also saw those principles through the many steps that eventually resulted in their adoption by vote of the membership of AEA.

The present volume is devoted to documenting and critiquing the resulting AEA *Guiding Principles for Evaluators*. In the first chapter, the task force members record the history of their efforts, with special attention to the most important conceptual issues that arose during the course of its deliberations. Many of those issues are intrinsic to the structure and functioning of the profession itself, and so will likely resurface continually over subsequent years and over subsequent efforts to revisit and revise the principles themselves. In the second chapter, the AEA *Guiding Principles for Evaluators* are presented in their official form, that is, the form in which they were approved by the AEA board of directors, accepted by vote of the AEA membership, and copyrighted by the AEA.

Throughout the rest of this volume, a number of evaluators from different settings, different countries, and different backgrounds discuss and critique both the strengths and weaknesses of the principles. These chapters fall into two categories. Chapters 3 through 7 discuss the principles at a very general level, addressing such matters as the nature of such principles and the rationale for them; the relationship of such general principles to more specific standards, both in theory and in the case of specific standards already developed; general objections that might be raised concerning principles, either of commission or omission. Chapters 8 through 11 focus on more specific issues, including problems of application that might arise for internal evaluators or private practice evaluators, the applicability of the principles in the context of international evaluation, and whether there is a need for more attention to multicultural issues in efforts such as the principles. In sum, Chapters 3 through 11 give evaluators considerable food for thought about the principles, and reflect exactly the kind of active, spirited dialogue about the nature of the evaluation profession that the task force and the AEA board hoped the principles would generate. Reflecting the need for continued dialogue of this type, the last chapter, Chapter 12, looks to the future, to the sorts of issues and activities that we should keep in mind for the continued use and development of these principles. The result of all these chapters, we hope, is a volume that both documents this piece of our history and points to the future that such efforts might bring in this continuing self-examination of what we do as professional evaluators.

William R. Shadish
Dianna L. Newman
Mary Ann Scheirer
Christopher Wye
Editors

WILLIAM R. SHADISH *is professor of psychology at the University of Memphis, outgoing editor-in-chief of* New Directions for Program Evaluation, *editor of* Evaluation Studies Review Annual *(Vol. 12, with Charles Reichardt), author of* Foundations of Program Evaluation *(with Thomas Cook and Laura Leviton), and the recipient of the 1994 AEA Lazarsfeld Award for Evaluation Theory.*

DIANNA L. NEWMAN *is associate professor specializing in program evaluation in the School of Education at the University at Albany/SUNY and director of the Evaluation Consortium at Albany.*

MARY ANN SCHEIRER *is a program evaluation consultant in Annandale, Virginia, following an extensive evaluation career in consulting firms and government agencies.*

CHRISTOPHER WYE *is director of the Program on Improving Government Performance and director of the Program on Ethics in the Public Service at the National Academy of Public Administration in Washington, D.C.*

This chapter presents some history relevant to the American Evaluation Association Guiding Principles for Evaluators, the processes used to create them, and some of the issues considered and controversies examined in the process.

Developing the Guiding Principles

William R. Shadish, Dianna L. Newman,
Mary Ann Scheirer, Christopher Wye

The American Evaluation Association (AEA), an organization devoted entirely to the study and practice of evaluation, recently completed a process of developing a code of guiding principles for evaluators. Given the importance of such codification in the development of a profession (Austin, 1981; Glassner, 1981), this chapter documents the processes by which diverse opinions were brought together, indicates the thoughts that went into the document, and points to issues that remain debatable.

In the past, professional evaluators have formally considered matters related to ethics. One such work is the *Standards for Program Evaluation* adopted by the Evaluation Research Society (1982). But those standards were never formally adopted by AEA after ERS merged with the Evaluation Network to form AEA in 1986. Another related work is by the Joint Committee on Standards for Educational Evaluation (see Sanders, this issue), which first published the *Standards for Evaluations of Educational Programs, Projects, and Materials* (1981), and more recently *The Program Evaluation Standards* (1994). AEA is represented on the Joint Committee and actively supports its work, but the sentiment prevailed that AEA wanted its own somewhat different document. One reason for this sentiment was that, as the main professional organization devoted to evaluation, AEA should articulate its own principles and not depend on a set of principles articulated by another organization. Also at work was the perception that the Joint Committee Standards grew out of educational evaluation more than other areas of evaluation.

Periodically AEA has discussed the merits of developing ethics and standards. The topic was pursued in discussions by the AEA board of directors, in numerous papers and symposia at the annual AEA convention, and in many published articles. But the present effort gained momentum during 1991–1992 when the AEA board vigorously debated the matter. To help resolve the matter productively, then AEA president David Cordray appointed a task force chaired by Peter Rossi. The following statement quoted from the minutes of the November 3, 1992, meeting summarizes the results of that task force:

> Dr. Rossi reported that his Task Force had considered three questions: 1) Is the concept needed; 2) If so, what should such "standards" look like; and 3) How to proceed. He reported that the Task Force concurred on the answers to those questions. Concerning item 1), some form of standards or more accurately, "guiding principles" are needed. . . . With respect to 2), the Task Force agreed that the "guiding principles" should not be specific or prescriptive; rather they would be general "guiding principles for evaluation practice." Finally, to proceed (item 3) the Task Force recommended that a follow-on Task Force be established, incorporating initially no more than 6–8 people, but including a wide range of evaluation practice and modes, as well as people who use evaluation. . . .
>
> The Board discussed a variety of issues associated with this recommendation. With respect to the purposes of such guiding principles, the Board agreed that it was not intended that they be used to police the organization but rather as a socialization and educational document, something generally to point to as the basic tenets of the profession. One Board member suggested the concept "criteria for excellence" as another way to describe the concept. Jim Sanders, attending the Board meeting as a Board Member–elect, reminded the Board of the history of AEA's involvement in the development of the Joint Committee on Evaluation Standards. It was noted that the debate on the issue needed to avoid the use of the word "standards" in describing the concept recommended by the Task Force, since that led to continuing confusion with the Joint Committee.
>
> The Board also discussed implementing recommendations with several comments expressing concern about whether the investment recommended . . . was the best way to proceed. In the end, several Board members (Mary Ann Scheirer, Chris Wye, Board Member–elect Dianna Newman, and Will Shadish, chair) volunteered to form an initial sub-group to draft some "guiding principles" to begin the discussions. . . . A MOTION WAS MADE, SECONDED, AND PASSED UNANIMOUSLY to authorize the volunteers to meet to draft guiding principles [pp. 9–10; emphasis in original text].

Both Rossi's task force and the AEA board were very clear from the start that the task to be done was to draft general *guiding principles* rather than highly specific *standards*, and the task force maintained that terminology throughout. Principles were understood to be conceptual rather than operational, giving guidance at the general level rather than at the level of how to make specific methodological or tactical decisions. The decision to focus on principles was supported by three reasons: principles seemed logically prerequisite to standards; developing principles could be accomplished more quickly and easily than developing standards; the focus would avoid an overlap with the task being done concurrently by the joint committee on revising its standards. Note that the task force members had diverse evaluation backgrounds—Shadish and Newman were academics, Scheirer was in private practice evaluation after a long time in contract-evaluation organizations, and Wye was in government administration—providing a representative cross-section of evaluation job settings. However, the recommendation of Rossi's group that the task force have representation by evaluation users seems to have been lost in the process.

Sequence of Events

During the course of its work, task force deliberations occurred by written correspondence; during lengthy conference calls on December 4 and 21, 1992, January 15, 1993, March 4, 1993, October 19, 1993, and December 16, 1993; and at the three meetings of the AEA board of directors in 1993, one of which occurred during the annual AEA convention. In addition, the task force sought and incorporated feedback from a variety of sources, by presenting interim results to the AEA board of directors at all three of its board meetings in 1993, by seeking feedback from all AEA members through a direct mailing of a draft of the Guiding Principles to them in September 1993, and by discussing the Guiding Principles at three symposia at the November 1993 annual meeting of AEA. At its January 1994 meeting, the AEA board of directors voted to accept the final draft of the Guiding Principles, terminated the task force, and authorized a membership vote on their adoption by AEA. The membership voted in favor of adopting the Guiding Principles in late summer, 1994.

Task force members agreed that a first step was to gather and consider relevant codes from other professional organizations. These included the *Government Auditing Standards* of the U.S. General Accounting Office (Comptroller General, 1988), the *Ethical Principles of Psychologists and Code of Conduct* (American Psychological Association, 1992), the federal regulations on *Protection of Human Subjects* (Protection of Human Subjects, 1983), the *Evaluation Research Society Standards for Program Evaluation* (Evaluation Research Society, 1982), the *Ethical Standards of the American Educational Research Association* (1992), the *Belmont Report* on ethical principles in biomedical and behavioral research (National Commission, 1979), the *Standards for Evaluations of Educational Programs, Projects, and Materials* (Joint Committee, 1981), and the *Principles of Professional Responsibility* of the American Anthropological Association (1990).

Task force members brought various prior experiences to bear on the tasks. Some of these reflected past work, such as Shadish's work on value theory (Shadish, Cook, and Leviton, 1991) or Scheirer's experience with ethical dilemmas in private practice, contract, and federal evaluation. Wye had been working on ethical issues at the National Academy of Public Administration. He circulated a draft chapter on that topic, and brought to the task a particular concern with the ethical dimensions of public service by public administrators. Newman circulated a memo with various proposals, and with attachments from her previously published works on ethical principles and standards (Brown and Newman, 1992).

All this occurred prior to the first conference call (December 4, 1992) and set the tone both for the task force's work style over the next year (very active) and for the conference call itself. During that call, the task force quickly agreed that the format used by the Belmont Report was worth using, given its brevity, its self-contained inclusion of a brief history, and its explication of assumptions, principles, and brief examples. The task force also agreed that the development of a brief statement of principles by the next January board meeting was feasible and desirable. Not surprisingly, there was considerable disagreement about exactly which principles from the many circulated documents were most appropriate for evaluators. Given these divergent opinions, task force members each agreed to draft a brief statement of proposed principles, with some justifications for each, by the next conference call (December 21, 1992).

From this first conference call, perhaps the most interesting conceptual issue that emerged concerned the *kind of profession* that evaluation is. For instance, is it most like medicine with its concern for helping the patient, most like auditing with its concern for accountability, or most like public administration with its concern for public service and the public good? The answer suggested the *kind of principles* that would be most appropriate. If evaluation is most like medicine, then the profession might emphasize principles aimed at benefiting clients. If evaluation is more like auditing, then the profession might emphasize principles ensuring the integrity of the process. The ethical principles of different kinds of professions are not entirely orthogonal, but they do not entirely overlap, either. Task force decisions about such assumptions were made explicit in the Preface (Section II) of the Guiding Principles, and implicitly in the principles themselves.

Early Drafts

Each task force member wrote a draft independently. One draft listed assumptions along with five proposed principles: Competence, Due Professional Care, Integrity, Respect for Stakeholders, and Value Explicitness. Another member proposed three principles—Objectivity, Performance, and Goodness—with pros and cons for each. The third proposed Objectivity, Integrity/Honesty, Respect for People, and Promoting the Public Good, each with elaborations. The fourth suggested five principles: Act to Benefit Others, Avoid Undue Harm, Respect Autonomy, Be Faithful or Loyal, and Promote Justice of Equity for All Participants; this draft was accompanied by pros and cons for each, and background assumptions. These drafts were mailed in the order just listed, and earlier drafts may have influenced later ones somewhat.

During the next two calls (December 21, 1992; January 15, 1993) most of the decisions were made that shaped the final draft. The basic format emerged: statements grouped into sections on background, assumptions, and principles.

The essence of the five final principles was agreed upon, most of the illustrations of each principle surfaced, and the task force identified areas of disagreement for future work.

Shortly after the December 21 call, the task force chair composed a draft document that integrated previous drafts. That document was discussed again in the January 15 call, revised, and sent to the AEA board for presentation at its January 29–31, 1993, meeting. That draft closely resembled the final document in general structure, except after each paragraph in the assumptions (Section II) and principles (Section III), a comment was inserted. If all task force members agreed on the paragraph, this always read "Comment: The Committee agreed on this statement"; otherwise, the comment summarized agreement and dissent. This format enabled keeping written track of disagreements and enabled writing an interim draft for the AEA board meeting.

Of the thirty-three paragraphs in that draft, twenty-eight yielded agreement. Of course, wording sometimes changed slightly over time, and some paragraphs were later combined to eliminate redundancy. This striking level of agreement reflects some consensus among task force members from diverse settings on many basic ethical issues.

Major Issues in Early Drafts

In five paragraphs of the draft, substantial disagreement existed. Although the task force reached some resolution on all of them, the resolution was not always fully satisfactory. These may be fundamental issues that arise from the structure and function of the profession. Hence, these issues may occur again in future discussions. Therefore, we now discuss these five.

To What Kinds of Evaluation Should the Principles Apply? The Guiding Principles are intended to apply to all kinds of evaluation. The task force did not agree on this initially. The first draft listed two versions of this statement, each version followed by a comment. The first version was:

> Statement: Evaluation is a broad community of professionals with varying interests, potentially encompassing the evaluation of programs, products, personnel, policy, performance, proposals, technology, research, theory, and even of evaluation itself. These principles are broadly intended to cover all these kinds of evaluation, except that personnel evaluation, which already has its own set of principles and standards, is not covered by these guidelines.

This comment followed:

> Comment: A majority of the Committee wanted principles that would encompass all evaluation, reflecting the nature and diversity of interests in the organization. However, problems arose because the application of these principles to things other than programs may be questionable. Personnel evaluation was

excluded, for example, because it was not clear that personnel evaluators owe primary obligation to the "public good" (Principle 5, version a) when they are employed by a private sector firm (e.g., General Motors). Excluding them solved that dilemma.

A related issue is that the Committee recognizes that most members of AEA may be most interested in program evaluation; and indeed, the Committee's own expertise lies mostly in that area. The critical perspective of other kinds of evaluators would be useful in exploring this issue further.

One Committee member who supported the notion of covering all types of evaluation wanted to delete the reference to excluding personnel evaluation, but also to delete the fifth guiding principle because that principle [5(1), the "public good" version] less clearly applies outside program evaluation. If version 5(2) ("obligations to the public") is adopted, it should apply to personnel evaluation, so one can again delete the exception for personnel evaluation above.

These comments identify a number of issues. One is the politics of balancing inter- and intra-organizational relationships: Would we be infringing on the turf of personnel evaluators who had their own standards? Would we alienate program evaluators by trying to be all things to all evaluators? A second issue is the role of the public good in evaluation, which might differ for different kinds of evaluators, thus complicating the task force's job of articulating these public interest issues. A third issue is that the methods and technical standards for doing diverse types of evaluation differ considerably, which might affect subsequent efforts to develop more specific standards for diverse types of evaluation.

To resolve such problems, one task force member proposed this alternative:

Statement: These guiding principles are focused primarily on program evaluation, because this is the major purpose for joining AEA among most of its members. However, evaluation in general is a broad community of professionals with varying interests, potentially encompassing the evaluation of programs, products, personnel, policy, performance, proposals, and technology. These principles may also cover these other types of evaluation, and we welcome dialogue and feedback from those whose emphasis is on other types of evaluation.

This was followed by its own comment:

Comment: A minority of the board [sic] was troubled by the attempt to cover all types of evaluation, preferring instead to cover mostly program evaluation since that is the major interest of most AEA members. Other organizations focus on other kinds of evaluation.

In the end, the task force wrote principles for all evaluators. The task force found a way to deal with the public interest issue in a manner that applied to all kinds of evaluation. Also, a document for AEA had to apply to all the many kinds of evaluators in AEA if the concept of evaluation was to be broadly applicable.

Implicit in the Guiding Principles is a hybrid model of evaluation in which it shares features of many professions but does not strictly follow any of them. For example, the Guiding Principles encourage some devotion to doing good and avoiding harm, as does medicine, at the same time recognizing that evaluation is like auditing in that it sometimes must report results that will cause harm to some persons or organizations.

Right to Autonomy. One initial draft referred to a principle of autonomy, the right of the evaluator and the evaluation client to make independent decisions:

> Statement: The right to autonomous judgments should be respected by both evaluators and clients. Evaluators' right to make judgments pertaining to design and technical matters should be respected by the client. The client's right to make judgments on issues related to selection of evaluator and legitimate use of information should be respected by the evaluator.

But some task force members objected:

> Comment: "Autonomous judgments" refers to the right to make the final decision, and carry the responsibility of making the final decision. It does not mean independent of discussion or without negotiation. The key issue here is to provide evaluators with the ability to say "I'm a professional, you hired me to do a job, trust me and let me do it." Clients, on the other hand, need to be able to say "We can hire whom we think will do the best job, and we ought to be able to use or not use the information as we think best." Note there is a difference between use, misuse and abuse of information; evaluators' responsibility to try to correct misuse of their work is already spelled out in principle 2e.
>
> The Committee unanimously agreed that supporting evaluators who are under pressure to produce a biased evaluation is desirable. A minority of the Committee felt that evaluators do not always have the rights to autonomy spelled out in this principle. For example, evaluators in the U.S. Census Bureau do not have the right to autonomously judge whether the design will include their preferred methods for estimating the undercount. As stated this principle gives them this right. Conversely, evaluators in academic settings almost certainly have the right (through academic freedom) to make a whole host of decisions bearing on matters that this principle would prohibit them from making. More generally, then, good evaluation can often involve negotiating everything, or nothing, depending on the setting; and evaluators have no compelling right to uniform autonomy on any topic. If the goal of this statement is to safeguard integrity, then this statement could be changed to reflect that better, for example: "Evaluators have the right to resist pressure to produce a biased evaluation."

The task force agreed that the Guiding Principles should protect evaluators from pressure to produce a biased evaluation. But a right to autonomy might not be appropriate for the employment settings in which some evaluators work. Thus, the task force adopted Guiding Principle III.C.6, a compromise between an unfettered right to autonomy and a more subservient evaluator role. This solution may be unsatisfactory. In their respective chapters in this issue, Chelimsky and Rossi chide the Guiding Principles for not supporting strongly enough the evaluator's right to autonomy. Conversely, the respective chapters by Lowell and Knott point out that III.C.6 may be too strong for some evaluators who may not have much organizational or economic freedom. Resolving this dilemma better is one task for the future.

Do Evaluators Have Any Obligation to the Public Interest? The key debates in the task force concerned evaluation and the public interest. The first statement formulated was:

> Statement: 5(1). Promoting the Public Good: The evaluator has obligations to the public at large that may transcend obligations to the immediate funding agency.

This was followed immediately by extensive commentary:

> Comment: The inclusion of this principle was controversial, leading to three positions. One Committee member wanted to delete this entire section (all of principle 5 and its substatements a through c); one wanted explicit reference to the "public good"; and two wanted reference to "obligations to the public" rather than to the "public good." Hence the Committee presents two possible versions of this principle, arguments for each, and arguments against the entire thrust of this section.
>
> Version 5(1) of this principle reflects the "public good" position. One Committee member felt this was the most important principle, superseding all others, and that reference to the public good was essential. This member argued that this principle codifies a key feature of the moral integrity of the profession, facilitating public trust in evaluation, providing evaluators with justification for refusing commissions or activities that run significantly counter to the public good, and increasing the likelihood that evaluation will contribute to the benefit of society. However, this principle also drew strong dissent because it elevates the public good above all other possible obligations that evaluators legitimately have. First, this may not clearly apply to evaluations that are not publicly funded, partly leading to the decision outlined in Principle IIf1 to exclude personnel evaluation in the private sector. Second, even within the public sector, major approaches to evaluation define quite different primary obligations than to the public good. For example, some evaluators say that our primary obligation is to (a) the consumer, (b) the full set of stakeholder interests, (c) the client who pays for the evaluation, (d) the program manager or policymaker, or (e) the disadvantaged. None of these is the same as the public good; and all are serious con-

tenders for the elevated status given to the "public good" here. Third, those who write about the public good have yet to agree on what it means, forwarding alternatives with very different implications. Fourth, this principle uses two phrases interchangeably—the "public at large" versus the "public good." Publicly funded evaluators may have obligations to consider interests of a broad array of stakeholders in the public at large; but such consideration does not lead in an obvious way to the public good. The phrases are not interchangeable.

Two Committee members wanted to substitute the following principle 5(2) to remedy these arguments. For reasons just outlined, one Committee member wanted to delete this entire section, except that reference to the public good be made under an earlier principle (e.g., 3c or 4e) as one of the many perspectives considered in the evaluation. This Committee member will also argue against the next version, 5(2).

An alternative version of this statement was:

> 5(2). Obligations to the Public. Evaluators supported by taxes or other publicly generated funds have obligations to the public at large that may transcend the immediate funding agency. The term public refers to all stakeholders, including researchers with interests in the topic area, any member of the population at large, the press, taxpayers, as well as clients, administrators, and funding agencies of the program.

This was followed by:

> Comment: This statement differs from the previous version in two ways. First, it adds the caveat "When supported by tax dollars or other publicly generated funds. . . ." This would eliminate the need to have the awkward exclusion of personnel evaluation in Section IIf1, and would help clarify the source and limitation of this obligation. Second, it drops mention of "public good" and replaces it with "public." The phrase "public good" has a substantial history of philosophical debate that has not reached agreement, and may carry more ambiguity than clarity if used in these AEA principles. By simply phrasing this principle in terms of the "public," we can refer to the concept of the multiple audiences for evaluations that exist in addition to the immediate client. The "public" obligations are in addition to the "private" obligations to the funding agent of the evaluation.
>
> A major reason why such evaluations ought to serve multiple public audiences is that many are ultimately funded by the public: by national, state, and local governments, and through publicly funded universities or schools. Even many private, non-profit organizations are funded by contributions from the general public. It is important to keep this principle in the AEA guiding principles in order to provide a basis for evaluators' claims to serve the interests of all major stakeholders. The proper role of an evaluator is not simply to provide data

to whoever is paying for it. In this respect, evaluation differs from market research.

One member of the Committee still argued for deleting this entire section. That member agreed that 5(2) solved some of the problems inherent in 5(1), especially by limiting its applicability to only publicly funded evaluations, and by removing difficulties defining the public good. But two objections remain. First, if the phrase "may transcend" in 5(2) is interpreted strictly to make this a primary obligation, then it does not remove the objection that this principle precludes evaluators from claiming a primary obligation to some more narrow set of stakeholders—those who evaluate drugs in the FDA, for example, could not claim primary obligation to protecting the patient. Second, if "may transcend" in 5(2) is interpreted more loosely as asserting the need to consider many points of view, of which the public is only one, then it is entirely redundant to previous calls in 3c or 4e to consider all views. Giving this principle *separate* status will inherently convey the impression that the interests of the "public" have a *special* status that *shall* transcend other interests.

If special mention is required of the role of the "public interest" in publicly funded evaluations as one of many views to be considered, this should occur as part of principle 4, or as part of a new principle 5 on obligations to clients and other stakeholders. That new principle might include (a) some previous statements referring to obligations to stakeholders, (b) a more explicit treatment of obligations to the funder, (c) mention of the role of the "public good" in publicly funded evaluation as one perspective to consider, and (d) acknowledgement that some of these obligations may conflict, without elevating one such obligation to uniform primary status.

The final draft of the Guiding Principles includes a principle entitled "Responsibilities for General and Public Welfare," reflecting a task force consensus that no evaluator can ever totally ignore the public interest. But a related issue required further attention.

Do Obligations to the Public Interest Supersede Other Obligations? If the public interest should play a role in evaluation, should that role take precedence over all other obligations? The initial draft contained a statement in favor of such a primacy:

> Evaluators as citizens carry the responsibility to seek the greater good of all members of society, rather than the immediate interests of a client or funding agency. (In this respect, evaluation is different from the professions of law and public relations.)

But this statement also drew strong dissenting commentary:

> Comment 1: This statement seeks to extend the basic "public good" principle by clarifying the source of the principle in civic duty, and by reminding evaluators

that certain "higher values" cannot be violated in the name of evaluation (the Nurenburg Trials on war crimes was cited as the prototype). Since it appeals to the "public good," it is subject to the critical comments already discussed about principle 5. It raises new problems, as well. First, it confuses a code of guiding principles for evaluators with a code of guiding principles for citizens. If the latter is a goal, much more should be added to this code; that is clearly impractical, and may be inappropriate since citizen duties are defined elsewhere as in the law. Second, the very premise of this statement is mistaken. Citizens do not necessarily carry the responsibility to seek the greater good. Under nearly all free marketplace economic theories, and under what may be the most commonly accepted theory of democracy applying to the U.S. (theories of pluralistic interest-group democracy), citizens are encouraged to pursue primarily their own self-interest. Third, to the extent that professions market services to clients, *legitimate* client interests have a strong claim to priority. To suggest otherwise misunderstands the nature of the economic and social basis of professions. Fourth, parenthetical comments about other professions open a topic too tangential to these guidelines without further development.

Comment 2: Responding to the above criticisms, two members of the Committee agreed to delete the phrase "as citizens" because this seems to go beyond the professional role of evaluators. This statement flows from the public nature of most of our profession, which is why it has similarities to the citizenship roles. But these Committee members wanted to keep the key point to establish with our profession, its funders, and other role partners that evaluators attempt to work for the good of all, rather than subscribing to more narrow role definitions of some other professions. In this respect, evaluation is not a service profession with obligations only to the immediate client (the funder). Many clients appear to believe that the evaluator's role is to serve the client's interests. This is an important reason for pointing out how we differ from other professions that do not focus primarily on serving clients. Our first guiding principle, above, articulates a generic statement of the basis of our professionalism: "The foundation of evaluation is to assess the merit or worth of the object being evaluated on the basis of empirical information." Note that this does not state that we provide information that will serve the interests of the client. In many cases, the interests of the client and broader stakeholder interests do not conflict. But in order to protect our claims to provide objective information for the use of a variety of publics, we need to include this principle in our ethical guidelines. We need to articulate here what kind of profession we are, or would like to become, in order to carry out such assessments, as a closing theme of the guidelines. If we do not emphasize good "science," then we do not provide good "service."

One Committee member still advocated deleting the entire principle. Deleting the phrase "as citizens" remedies one objection, but leaves the rest, and substitutes a new problem—what rationale now justifies the assertion that evaluators are responsible for seeking the greater good of all members? The rationale proposed in this comment attempts to connect the "greater good" with objectivity and good science. The connection is tenuous at best. Evaluators can clearly do scientifically good, objective work for a narrowly defined stakeholder interest. Consideration of many interests, including the general good, is a generally laudable aspiration; but the conduct of evaluation practice is too contextually bound to accommodate a mandate to always put the public good above all other interests.

Debate eventually led to two separate statements in the final Guiding Principles. Statement III.E.4 acknowledges that evaluators have a special obligation to respond to the legitimate needs of clients for legal and economic reasons. But III.E.4 also notes that client needs can conflict with other obligations, and suggests some solutions to such conflicts. Statement III.E.5 acknowledges that the obligations of evaluators also encompass the public interest and good. But it neither makes those obligations transcendant nor allows any evaluator to ignore the public interest entirely.

Freedom of Information. Information promotes the public's ability to act in its own interest. Freedom of information, therefore, is closely tied to the public interest. Hence the first illustration of the initial public interest principle noted:

> Statement: Since freedom of information is essential in a democracy, evaluators should attempt to report their findings to all stakeholders, and should not keep secret or selectively communicate their findings.

This was followed by:

> Comment: The basic principle of a free flow of information to facilitate democracy is agreed upon by the Committee. But this statement goes much further. It prohibits selective communication, but it is often good practice to tailor evaluation reports to the needs of each stakeholder group to facilitate use. Also, because dissemination of reports is tied intimately to use, this statement contradicts principle 1d granting clients the right to autonomous control on use. A more innocuous phrasing might be that "evaluators should ensure that all stakeholders have access to findings and reports in which they have a legitimate interest."

A version of this statement was endorsed in the final Guiding Principles (III.E.3). Some evaluators criticized the statement (see the chapter by Knott in this issue) because good reasons sometimes exist not to inform all stakeholders about the results of an evaluation, especially if more harm than good might occur.

Other Matters of Note. Certain careful phrasing in the Guiding Principles might not be obvious to the reader. Many statements are hedged with "where appropriate," "barring compelling reason to the contrary," or "within reasonable limits" because most general statements will have legitimate exceptions. Such exceptions were often the subject of feedback by AEA members, often with vivid examples of the dilemma claimed. Such qualifiers can make statements vague, so good evaluator judgment must be the final arbiter.

The Guiding Principles do not explicitly define evaluation, reflecting disagreement in the field. But II.B states: "The common ground is that evaluators aspire to construct and provide the best possible information that might bear on the value of whatever is being evaluated. The principles are intended to foster that primary aim." The latter sentence implies that the five Guiding Principles are not generally ends in themselves, but means to the end of obtaining the best evaluation. Sometimes a Guiding Principle can be an end itself, as in guarding against extreme violations of the public good.

The first Guiding Principle, Systematic Inquiry, prompted debate about the words it used, like data, objective, or empirical. Such words seemed provocative to some evaluators. Perhaps evaluators have lost a common language for referring to this part of the work and for determining whether or not we aspire to be "scientific" in any substantial sense of the word. We seem to agree that we are doing something more than gossip, but disagree about what that something is. This issue arose partly from the quantitative-qualitative debates that were prominent in AEA when the task force was working (for example, Lincoln, 1991; Lincoln and Guba, 1992; Sechrest, 1992; Sechrest, Babcock, and Smith, 1993).

The phrasing of Section III.D.2 was also quite careful: "evaluators should seek to maximize the benefits and reduce any unnecessary harms that might occur, provided this will not compromise the integrity of the evaluation findings." This is not the same as doing good and avoiding harm, for some evaluations must cause harm to some stakeholder interests; rather, it calls for carefully assessing harms that might be done, and then trying to reduce those that might be unnecessary. But this assessment must keep the larger goal in mind, to produce the best evaluation, even if it results in some harm.

Evolving the Final Draft

In addition to the board's comments, feedback was generated by a mailing of the Guiding Principles to the entire AEA membership in September 1993 and through three symposia at the November 1993 AEA annual meeting. From this feedback, several themes stand out. First, evaluators noted aspects of the Guiding Principles that were problematic in their specific work setting. For example, internal evaluators noted that they rarely had the freedom to decline an evaluation. The task force modified the Guiding Principles accordingly because it does no good to ask evaluators to do the impossible. Inevitably, however, such problems could not be accommodated fully without gutting particular statements, which the task force usually rejected.

Second, some evaluators asked for specific yardsticks for practice. Some critics asked for standards rather than principles, and others criticized the use of vague phrases like "where appropriate." The AEA board specifically instructed the task force to create principles, not standards, so the task force acted on few such requests. In contrast, some evaluators expressed concern that the Guiding Principles would be used to sanction evaluators. As Sections II.G and II.H note, this is not the purpose of the principles.

Third, some commentators saw the principles as too much a compromise between specificity and generality, between the needs of evaluators and their clients, or between flexibility and firmness (see the chapter by Rossi in this issue). The appropriateness of such compromises should be grist for the mill of future revisions. The fourth theme from the feedback concerned the user-friendliness of the Guiding Principles. One group of commentators objected that the labels were not memorable nor was the introduction engaging. Others noted the use of jargon and too high a reading comprehension level. The task force tried various remedies, but a new draft would benefit from the skills of a professional writer.

Another concern was the legal ramifications of the Guiding Principles. The task force sought legal counsel, but the opinions obtained were mixed. Sections of the Guiding Principles (II.D, II.G, II.H) note that AEA intends these principles to stimulate debate but not to be used to monitor or sanction the practices of individual evaluators. The Ethical Standards published by the American Educational Research Association (1992) have a similar disclaimer:

> The Ethical Standards of the American Educational Research Association were developed and, in June 1992, adopted by AERA to be an educational document, to stimulate collegial debate, and to evoke voluntary compliance by moral persuasion. Accordingly, it is not the intention of the Association to monitor adherence to the Standards or to investigate allegations of violations to the Code [p. 23].

A revision of the Guiding Principles should consider adding such a statement.

In a last conference call (December 16, 1993), the task force agreed upon final wording, recommended that the Guiding Principles be submitted to the AEA membership for vote, and recommended that the AEA standing ethics committee carry on the work of the task force. The AEA board of directors approved all of these proposals at its January 1994 meeting. The task force was disbanded, the membership voted to adopt the Guiding Principles in late summer, 1994, and the ethics committee assumed responsibility for developing plans for dissemination, utilization, and periodic review of the principles, and providing forums for discussion of ethical issues. Newman (see the chapter in this issue) describes some of the issues that the committee, and the profession of evaluation generally, must face as it pursues these matters.

Summary

In retrospect, then, the process started by the appointment of the task force on guiding principles for evaluators led to considerable progress on these issues in just a little over one year. The task force was able to develop a set of guiding principles that demonstrated considerable agreement about the principles to which the profession should aspire. That in itself is no mean feat. Even more felicitous, the AEA membership seemed to welcome this development both professionally and intellectually. We take all this to be a mark of the continued professional and intellectual maturing of evaluation.

References

American Anthropological Association. *Statements on Ethics: Principles of Professional Responsibility.* American Anthropological Association. Arlington, Va.: American Anthropological Association, 1990.

American Educational Research Association. "Ethical Standards." *Educational Researcher,* 1992, *21,* 23–26.

American Psychological Association. "Ethical Principles of Psychologists and Code of Conduct." *American Psychologist,* 1992, *47,* 1597–1611.

Austin, D. "The Development of Clinical Sociology." *Journal of Applied Behavioral Science,* 1981, *17,* 347–350.

Brown, R. D., and Newman, D. L. "Ethical Principles and Evaluation Standards: Do They Match?" *Evaluation Review* 1992, *16,* 650–663.

Comptroller General. *Government Auditing Standards.* Stock no. 020-000-00243-3. Washington, D.C.: U.S. Government Printing Office, 1988.

Evaluation Research Society Standards Committee. "Evaluation Research Society Standards for Program Evaluation." In P. H. Rossi (ed.), *Standards for Evaluation Practice.* New Directions for Program Evaluation, no. 15. San Francisco: Jossey-Bass, 1982.

Glassner, B. "Clinical Applications of Sociology in Health Care." *Journal of Applied Behavioral Science,* 1981, *17,* 330–346.

Joint Committee on Standards for Educational Evaluation. *Standards for Evaluations of Educational Programs, Projects, and Materials.* New York: McGraw-Hill, 1981.

Joint Committee on Standards for Educational Evaluation. *The Program Evaluation Standards.* Newbury Park, Calif.: Sage, 1994.

Lincoln, Y. S. "The Arts and Sciences of Program Evaluation." *Evaluation Practice,* 1991, *12,* 1–7.

Lincoln, Y. S., and Guba, E. G. "In Response to Lee Sechrest's 1991 AEA Presidential Address: 'Roots: Back to Our First Generation.'" *Evaluation Practice,* 1992, *13,* 165–169.

National Commission for the Protection of Human Subjects of Biomedical and Behavioral Research. *The Belmont Report: Ethical Principles and Guidelines for the Protection of Human Subjects of Research.* OPRR Reports; FR Doc. 79-12065. Washington, D.C.: U.S. Government Printing Office, 1979.

Protection of Human Subjects. 45 CFR 46, 1983.

Rossi, P. H. (ed.). *Standards for Evaluation Practice.* New Directions for Program Evaluation, no. 15. San Francisco: Jossey-Bass, 1982.

Shadish, W. R., Cook, T. D., and Leviton, L. C. *Foundations of Program Evaluation.* Newbury Park, Calif.: Sage, 1991.

Sechrest, L. "Roots: Back to Our First Generation." *Evaluation Practice,* 1992, *13,* 1–7.

Sechrest, L., Babcock, J., and Smith, B. "An invitation to methodological pluralism." *Evaluation Practice,* 1993, *14,* 227–236.

WILLIAM R. SHADISH *is professor of psychology at the University of Memphis, outgoing editor-in-chief of* New Directions for Program Evaluation, *editor of* Evaluation Studies Review Annual *(Vol. 12, with Charles Reichardt), author of* Foundations of Program Evaluation *(with Thomas Cook and Laura Leviton), and the recipient of the 1994 AEA Lazarsfeld Award for Evaluation Theory.*

DIANNA L. NEWMAN *is associate professor specializing in program evaluation in the School of Education at the University at Albany/SUNY and director of the Evaluation Consortium at Albany.*

MARY ANN SCHEIRER *is a program evaluation consultant in Annandale, Virginia, following an extensive evaluation career in consulting firms and government agencies.*

CHRISTOPHER WYE *is director of the Program on Improving Government Performance and director of the Program on Ethics in the Public Service at the National Academy of Public Administration in Washington, D.C.*

Presented here is the version of the American Evaluation Association Guiding Principles for Evaluators *that was approved and copyrighted by the AEA board of directors and subsequently adopted by vote of the AEA membership.*

Guiding Principles for Evaluators

American Evaluation Association, Task Force on Guiding Principles for Evaluators

I. Introduction
   A. *Background*: In 1986, the Evaluation Network (ENet) and the Evaluation Research Society (ERS) merged to create the American Evaluation Association. ERS had previously adopted a set of standards for program evaluation (published in *New Directions for Program Evaluation* in 1982), and both organizations had lent support to work of other organizations about evaluation guidelines. However, none of these standards or guidelines were officially adopted by AEA, nor were any other ethics, standards, or guiding principles put into place. Over the ensuing years, the need for such guiding principles has been discussed by both the AEA Board and the AEA membership. Under the presidency of David Cordray in 1992, the AEA Board appointed a temporary committee chaired by Peter Rossi to examine whether AEA should address this matter in more detail. That committee issued a report to the AEA Board on November 4, 1992, recommending that AEA should pursue this matter further. The Board followed that recommendation and on that date created a Task Force to develop a draft of guiding principles for evaluators. The AEA Board specifically instructed the Task Force to develop general guiding principles rather than specific standards of practice. This report summarizes the Task Force's response to the charge.
   B. *Process*: Task Force members reviewed relevant documents from other professional societies, and then independently prepared and circulated drafts of material for use in this report. Initial and subsequent drafts

---

Copyright 1994, American Evaluation Association. Reprinted with permission.

(compiled by the Task Force chair) were discussed during conference calls, with revisions occurring after each call. Progress reports were presented at every AEA Board meeting during 1993. In addition, a draft of the guidelines was mailed to all AEA members in September 1993 requesting feedback, and three symposia at the 1993 AEA annual conference were used to discuss and obtain further feedback. The Task Force considered all this feedback in a December 1993 conference call and prepared a final draft in January 1994. This draft was presented and approved for membership vote at the January 1994 AEA Board meeting.
C. *Resulting Principles*: Given the diversity of interests and employment settings represented on the Task Force, it is noteworthy that Task Force members reached substantial agreement about the following five principles. The order of these principles does not imply priority among them; priority will vary by situation and evaluator role.
1. *Systematic Inquiry*: Evaluators conduct systematic, data-based inquiries about whatever is being evaluated.
2. *Competence*: Evaluators provide competent performance to stakeholders.
3. *Integrity/Honesty*: Evaluators ensure the honesty and integrity of the entire evaluation process.
4. *Respect for People*: Evaluators respect the security, dignity, and self-worth of the respondents, program participants, clients, and other stakeholders with whom they interact.
5. *Responsibilities for General and Public Welfare*: Evaluators articulate and take into account the diversity of interests and values that may be related to the general and public welfare.

These five principles are elaborated in Section III of this document.
D. *Recommendation for Continued Work*: The Task Force also recommends that the AEA Board establish and support a mechanism for the continued development and dissemination of these Guiding Principles.

II. Preface: Assumptions Concerning Development of Principles
  A. Evaluation is a profession composed of persons with varying interests, potentially encompassing but not limited to the evaluation of programs, products, personnel, policy, performance, proposals, technology, research, theory, and even of evaluation itself. These principles are broadly intended to cover all kinds of evaluation.
  B. Based on differences in training, experience, and work settings, the profession of evaluation encompasses diverse perceptions about the primary purpose of evaluation. These include but are not limited to the following: bettering products, personnel, programs, organizations, governments, consumers, and the public interest; contributing to informed decision making and more enlightened change; precipitating needed change;

empowering all stakeholders by collecting data from them and engaging them in the evaluation process; and experiencing the excitement of new insights. Despite that diversity, the common ground is that evaluators aspire to construct and provide the best possible information that might bear on the value of whatever is being evaluated. The principles are intended to foster that primary aim.

C. The intention of the Task Force was to articulate a set of principles that should guide the professional practice of evaluators, and that should inform evaluation clients and the general public about the principles they can expect to be upheld by professional evaluators. Of course, no statement of principles can anticipate all situations that arise in the practice of evaluation. However, principles are not just guidelines for reaction when something goes wrong or when a dilemma is found. Rather, principles should proactively guide the behaviors of professionals in everyday practice.

D. The purpose of documenting guiding principles is to foster continuing development of the profession of evaluation, and the socialization of its members. The principles are meant to stimulate discussion and to provide a language for dialogue about the proper practice and application of evaluation among members of the profession, sponsors of evaluation, and others interested in evaluation.

E. The five principles proposed in this document are not independent, but overlap in many ways. Conversely, sometimes these principles will conflict, so that evaluators will have to choose among them. At such times evaluators must use their own values and knowledge of the setting to determine the appropriate response. Whenever a course of action is unclear, evaluators should solicit the advice of fellow evaluators about how to resolve the problem before deciding how to proceed.

F. These principles are intended to replace any previous work on standards, principles, or ethics adopted by ERS or ENet, the two predecessor organizations to AEA. These principles are the official position of AEA on these matters.

G. Each principle is illustrated by a number of statements to amplify the meaning of the overarching principle and to provide guidance for its application. These statements are illustrations. They are not meant to include all possible applications of that principle, nor to be viewed as rules that provide the basis for sanctioning violators.

H. These principles are not intended to be or to replace standards supported by evaluators or by the other disciplines in which evaluators participate. Specifically, AEA supports the effort to develop standards for educational evaluation by the Joint Committee on Standards for Educational Evaluation, of which AEA is a cosponsor.

I. These principles were developed in the context of Western cultures, particularly the United States, and so may reflect the experiences of that context. The relevance of these principles may vary across other cultures, and across subcultures within the United States.

J. These principles are part of an evolving process of self-examination by the profession and should be revisited on a regular basis. Mechanisms might include officially sponsored reviews of principles at annual meetings and other forums for harvesting experience with the principles and their application. On a regular basis, but at least every five years from the date they initially take effect, these principles ought to be examined for possible review and revision. In order to maintain association-wide awareness and relevance, all AEA members are encouraged to participate in this process.

III. The Principles

A. *Systematic Inquiry*: Evaluators conduct systematic, data-based inquiries about whatever is being evaluated.
 1. Evaluators should adhere to the highest appropriate technical standards in conducting their work, whether that work is quantitative or qualitative in nature, so as to increase the accuracy and credibility of the evaluative information they produce.
 2. Evaluators should explore with the client the shortcomings and strengths both of the various evaluation questions it might be productive to ask, and the various approaches that might be used for answering those questions.
 3. When presenting their work, evaluators should communicate their methods and approaches accurately and in sufficient detail to allow others to understand, interpret, and critique their work. They should make clear the limitations of an evaluation and its results. Evaluators should discuss in a contextually appropriate way those values, assumptions, theories, methods, results, and analyses that *significantly* affect the interpretation of the evaluative findings. These statements apply to all aspects of the evaluation, from its initial conceptualization to the eventual use of findings.

B. *Competence*: Evaluators provide competent performance to stakeholders.
 1. Evaluators should possess (or, here and elsewhere as appropriate, ensure that the evaluation team possesses) the education, abilities, skills, and experience appropriate to undertake the tasks proposed in the evaluation.
 2. Evaluators should practice within the limits of their professional training and competence and should decline to conduct evaluations that fall substantially outside those limits. When declining the commission or request is not feasible or appropriate, evaluators should make clear any significant limitations on the evaluation that might result. Evaluators should make every effort to gain the competence directly or

through the assistance of others who possess the required expertise.
3. Evaluators should continually seek to maintain and improve their competencies, in order to provide the highest level of performance in their evaluations. This continuing professional development might include formal coursework and workshops, self-study, evaluations of one's own practice, and working with other evaluators to learn from their skills and expertise.

C. *Integrity/Honesty:* Evaluators ensure the honesty and integrity of the entire evaluation process.
1. Evaluators should negotiate honestly with clients and relevant stakeholders concerning the costs, tasks to be undertaken, limitations of methodology, scope of results likely to be obtained, and uses of data resulting from a specific evaluation. It is primarily the evaluator's responsibility to initiate discussion and clarification of these matters, not the client's.
2. Evaluators should record all changes made in the originally negotiated project plans, and the reasons why the changes were made. If those changes would significantly affect the scope and likely results of the evaluation, the evaluator should inform the client and other important stakeholders in a timely fashion (barring good reason to the contrary, before proceeding with further work) of the changes and their likely impact.
3. Evaluators should seek to determine, and where appropriate be explicit about, their own, their clients', and other stakeholders' interests concerning the conduct and outcomes of an evaluation (including financial, political, and career interests).
4. Evaluators should disclose any roles or relationships they have concerning whatever is being evaluated that might pose a significant conflict of interest with their role as an evaluator. Any such conflict should be mentioned in reports of the evaluation results.
5. Evaluators should not misrepresent their procedures, data, or findings. Within reasonable limits, they should attempt to prevent or correct any substantial misuses of their work by others.
6. If evaluators determine that certain procedures or activities seem likely to produce misleading evaluative information or conclusions, they have the responsibility to communicate their concerns, and the reasons for them, to the client (the one who funds or requests the evaluation). If discussions with the client do not resolve these concerns, so that a misleading evaluation is then implemented, the evaluator may legitimately decline to conduct the evaluation if that is feasible and appropriate. If not, the evaluator should consult colleagues or relevant stakeholders about other proper ways to proceed (options might include, but are not limited to, discussions at a higher level, a dissenting cover letter or appendix, or refusal to sign the final document).

7. Barring compelling reason to the contrary, evaluators should disclose all sources of financial support for an evaluation, and the source of the request for the evaluation.

D. *Respect for People*: Evaluators respect the security, dignity and self-worth of the respondents, program participants, clients, and other stakeholders with whom they interact.

1. Where applicable, evaluators must abide by current professional ethics and standards regarding risks, harms, and burdens that might be engendered to those participating in the evaluation; regarding informed consent for participation in evaluation; and regarding informing participants about the scope and limits of confidentiality. Examples of such standards include federal regulations about protection of human subjects, or the ethical principles of such associations as the American Anthropological Association, the American Educational Research Association, or the American Psychological Association. Although this principle is not intended to extend the applicability of such ethics and standards beyond their current scope, evaluators should abide by them where it is feasible and desirable to do so.
2. Because justified negative or critical conclusions from an evaluation must be explicitly stated, evaluations sometimes produce results that harm client or stakeholder interests. Under this circumstance, evaluators should seek to maximize the benefits and reduce any unnecessary harms that might occur, provided this will not compromise the integrity of the evaluation findings. Evaluators should carefully judge when the benefits from doing the evaluation or in performing certain evaluation procedures should be foregone because of the risks or harms. Where possible, these issues should be anticipated during the negotiation of the evaluation.
3. Knowing that evaluations often will negatively affect the interests of some stakeholders, evaluators should conduct the evaluation and communicate its results in a way that clearly respects the stakeholders' dignity and self-worth.
4. Where feasible, evaluators should attempt to foster the social equity of the evaluation, so that those who give to the evaluation can receive some benefits in return. For example, evaluators should seek to ensure that those who bear the burdens of contributing data and incurring any risks are doing so willingly, and that they have full knowledge of, and maximum feasible opportunity to obtain any benefits that may be produced from the evaluation. When it would not endanger the integrity of the evaluation, respondents or program participants should be informed if and how they can receive services to which they are otherwise entitled without participating in the evaluation.

5. Evaluators have the responsibility to identify and respect differences among participants, such as differences in their culture, religion, gender, disability, age, sexual orientation, and ethnicity, and to be mindful of potential implications of these differences when planning, conducting, analyzing, and reporting their evaluations.

E. *Responsibilities for General and Public Welfare*: Evaluators articulate and take into account the diversity of interests and values that may be related to the general and public welfare.

1. When planning and reporting evaluations, evaluators should consider including important perspectives and interests of the full range of stakeholders in the object being evaluated. Evaluators should carefully consider the justification when omitting important value perspectives or the views of important groups.
2. Evaluators should consider not only the immediate operations and outcomes of whatever is being evaluated, but also the broad assumptions, implications, and potential side effects of it.
3. Freedom of information is essential in a democracy. Hence, barring compelling reason to the contrary, evaluators should allow all relevant stakeholders to have access to evaluative information and should actively disseminate that information to stakeholders if resources allow. If different evaluation results are communicated in forms that are tailored to the interests of different stakeholders, those communications should ensure that each stakeholder group is aware of the existence of the other communications. Communications that are tailored to a given stakeholder should always include all important results that may bear on interests of that stakeholder. In all cases, evaluators should strive to present results as clearly and simply as accuracy allows so that clients and other stakeholders can easily understand the evaluation process and results.
4. Evaluators should maintain a balance between client needs and other needs. Evaluators necessarily have a special relationship with the client who funds or requests the evaluation. By virtue of that relationship, evaluators must strive to meet legitimate client needs whenever it is feasible and appropriate to do so. However, that relationship can also place evaluators in difficult dilemmas when client interests conflict with other interests, or when client interests conflict with the obligation of evaluators for systematic inquiry, competence, integrity, and respect for people. In these cases, evaluators should explicitly identify and discuss the conflicts with the client and relevant stakeholders, resolve them when possible, determine whether continued work on the evaluation is advisable if the conflicts cannot be resolved, and make clear any significant limitations on the evaluation that might result if the conflict is not resolved.
5. Evaluators have obligations that encompass the public interest and

good. These obligations are especially important when evaluators are supported by publicly generated funds; but clear threats to the public good should never be ignored in any evaluation. Because the public interest and good are rarely the same as the interests of any particular group (including those of the client or funding agency), evaluators will usually have to go beyond an analysis of particular stakeholder interests when considering the welfare of society as a whole.

The members of the AEA task force on Guiding Principles for Evaluators were Dianna L. Newman, Mary Ann Scheirer, William R. Shadish (task force chair), and Christopher Wye.

DIANNA L. NEWMAN *is associate professor specializing in program evaluation in the School of Education at the University at Albany/SUNY and director of the Evaluation Consortium at Albany.*

MARY ANN SCHEIRER *is a program evaluation consultant in Annandale, Virginia, following an extensive evaluation career in consulting firms, and government agencies.*

WILLIAM R. SHADISH *is professor of psychology at the University of Memphis, outgoing editor-in-chief of* New Directions for Program Evaluation, *editor of* Evaluation Studies Review Annual *(Vol. 12, with Charles Reichardt), author of* Foundations of Program Evaluation *(with Thomas Cook and Laura Leviton), and the recipient of the 1994 AEA Lazarsfeld Award for Evaluation Theory.*

CHRISTOPHER WYE *is director of the Program on Improving Government Performance and director of the Program on Ethics in the Public Service at the National Academy of Public Administration in Washington, D.C.*

The American Evaluation Association's succinct Guiding Principles for Evaluators quietly establish new boundaries for addressing ethical problems of the profession.

Principled Evaluation: A Critique of the AEA Guiding Principles

Ernest R. House

It is difficult to write intelligently about ethics and values. One reason is that ethical problems are manifested only in particular concrete cases, and endorsement of general principles sometimes seems platitudinous or irrelevant. Ethical concerns become interesting only in conflicted cases, and it is often the balance of principles that is crucial rather than the principles themselves.

Another difficulty in discussing ethics rationally is the value-free tradition of the social sciences in the United States. During the first half of the twentieth century, some social scientists were persecuted and dismissed from their jobs because of their unpopular social and political beliefs, such as endorsing socialist ideas or advocating laws to abolish child labor (Ross, 1991). Those serving on university governing boards and those contributing money to universities sometimes took strong exception to such views, even to the point of attacking and sacking individual professors.

This situation attracted social scientists to value-free positions as well as to quantitative methods that could not be accused of being biased by improper values. After all, if one is counting or reporting social conditions rather than evaluating them, how could one be held responsible? Philosophic positions that advocated value-free science and the separation of fact and value, such as logical positivism, were accepted readily. Values had little to do with scientific practice, in this view.

The Cold War again put social scientists at risk for their values. Few remember the constrained social and political environment of Sen. Joseph McCarthy and the House Un-American Activities Committee in the 1950s (Halberstam, 1993). In the 1960s, Vietnam War protests legitimized antigovernment sentiments and polarized academics between those who wanted to address value questions and those who adhered to value neutrality. Discussions tended to be polemical, no surprise perhaps, because there had been little opportunity to consider values in a disciplined manner previously. Developing a value position for a profession in such conditions seemed futile. However, with the Cold War over, perhaps it is possible to have a disciplined ethical discourse that evaluators can accept without fear of political repercussions.

Another difficulty in the rational discussion of ethics and values is that such discussion increases the possibility of conflict within a professional evaluation community that is sometimes factionalized along methodological lines. Can people agree on ethics and values when they cannot agree on methods for collecting data? Ethical considerations could splinter the community again just as the quantitative-qualitative rift is healing. A few highly regarded evaluation theorists, such as Bob Stake and Lee Cronbach, have said on occasions that we should not have such principles. Principles will not supply answers to tough questions, or cannot do justice to the complexity of actual situations.

The aim should be to begin an open, ongoing dialogue about ethical problems that evaluators face and to provide the legitimacy and occasion for discussing such issues in professional forums. One benefit of doing so is to bring the evaluation community together in an act of mutual identity while offering the possibility of improving the performance of evaluators as they face ethical dilemmas. We have such problems and should talk about them, even if we cannot solve them. If we talked only about things we can solve, it would be a quiet world indeed.

Although the standards for *educational* evaluators are quite good, they do not represent the evaluation community as a whole because most AEA members had no role in defining them (Joint Committee, 1980, 1988, 1994; Stufflebeam, 1991). Also, the earlier Evaluation Research Society standards (1982) need to be recast for a different membership. Engagement of the community is critical in such a process, and the AEA task force has done an admirable job of keeping the process open. So having attested to the difficulty of such an endeavor, I will critique the principles by testing them against common ethical fallacies in evaluation.

Ethical Fallacies of Evaluation

The ethics of evaluation studies are a subset of ethics or morality in general, but ethics applied to professional problems. According to Sieber (1980, p. 52), "If there were a field of applied ethics for program evaluation, that field would study how to choose morally right actions and maximize the value of one's work in program evaluation. It would examine the kinds of dilemmas that arise in program evaluation; it would establish Principles for anticipating and resolving certain ethical problems and encompass a subarea of scientific methodology for performing evaluation that satisfies both scientific and ethical requirements; and it would consider ways to promote ethical character in program evaluators."

What ethical problems do evaluators face? First, they exercise powers over people that can injure self-esteem, damage reputations, and stunt careers. Often these people are not able to defend or express their own interests. Second, evaluators are engaged in relationships in which they themselves are vulnerable to people awarding future work. Some people evaluators deal with are influential within the evaluators' own career realm. Also, evaluators come from the same social classes and educational backgrounds as those who sponsor the evaluations and run the programs. These factors multiply ethical hazards.

Some ethical mistakes occur so frequently that they deserve the label of ethical fallacies, including clientism, contractualism, methodologicalism, relativism, and pluralism/elitism.

Clientism. Clientism is the claim that doing whatever the client wants or whatever is to the benefit of the client is ethically correct. The analogy is with the doctor-patient relationship, in which all the doctor must do is attend to the patient's welfare. However, this is not the client relationship evaluators engage in. To take an extreme example, what if the client is Adolph Eichmann, and he wants the evaluator to increase the efficiency of his concentration camps? This situation is not as far-fetched as one might think, given the documented abuse of radiation research during the Cold War.

Evaluators must accept responsibilities beyond duty to client, as medical doctors do. If a doctor determined that a client with a dangerous virus would be best off if allowed to move freely in society, but that the virus was highly contagious and would infect other people, the doctor's duty must be to the health of the community as a whole. The same is true for evaluators. Service to the client, while highly desirable, is insufficient as an ethical basis. There must be concern for the public welfare at some point. Of course, service to the client and concern for the public good do not conflict ordinarily, but the evaluator must be aware that conflict is possible.

Contractualism. Another fallacy is that the evaluator must follow the written contract absolutely, whatever the situation. Following the agreement is the correct thing for the evaluator to do most of the time, but not in every circumstance. Considerations arise beyond the contract. For example, what if the evaluator discovers a serious human rights abuse, but such a contingency was not part of the contract? The lack of contractual authority does not alleviate moral responsibility. As currently conceived, professional ethics in program evaluation is a contractual ethics predicated on a fair evaluation agreement (House and Care, 1979). This is not true in product evaluation, however, in which organizations like Consumer's Union evaluate products without agreements between producer and evaluator. Much can be said for a contractual ethics, but there are limits.

Methodologicalism. Some evaluators, especially those holding a traditional social science view of evaluation, believe that following acceptable research methods is in itself sufficient for ethical performance. This position was popular when facts and values were conceived as separate entities and the social scientist's responsibility was to produce value-free facts, thus avoiding ethical problems altogether. In truth, ethical considerations extend beyond proper methodology, and methodologies frequently lead to ethical problems (Conner, 1980; Sieber, 1982).

For example, the ethical dilemma of choosing some subjects for experimental treatment and not others has been discussed extensively. Qualitative methods in particular lead to a host of ethical problems because the evaluator is likely to uncover personal information which could be damaging to participants. What goes into the evaluation report and what stays out? The decision is as much ethical as methodological. And methods alone, of whatever type, cannot address all such issues.

Relativism. Another fallacy is that the evaluator's responsibility is to collect data from participants in the study and accept everyone's opinions equally. Knowledge and judgments are strictly relative, in this view. Again, what if Adolph Eichmann is a member of the group? Are we to accept his opinions equally with everyone else's and accord them full ethical standing? Obviously not. Considerations beyond equality of individual and group opinions must come into play.

This is a confused issue because it is confounded with cultural relativism, which contends that things from other cultures must be accepted as being equal or at least acceptable. However, there is no reason even from a multicultural perspective to take the view that all actions are equal or acceptable just because they originate in another culture. It is common in East Indian culture to burn the bride because she brings insufficient dowry to the marriage. But surely one cannot accept bride-burning because it is part of Indian culture. Nor should we accept the reduced status of women in some Muslim countries because it is part of their culture. It is possible to make judgments across cultures on some occasions, which is not the same as saying that everyone should speak English.

Pluralism/Elitism. The pluralism/elitism fallacy is similar to relativism in that the evaluator collects the opinions and values of various participants in the program—for example, decision makers, administrators, legislators, participants—and puts them together in some unspecified way. How these values and opinions are adjudicated is not clear. This is probably the most common position in evaluation, but one riddled with ethical difficulties. The usual outcome of such an approach is to give the powerful a priority voice in the evaluation because it is mostly the powerful rather than the powerless or voiceless whose opinions and values have been solicited and used. Evaluators must adopt a more democratic stand than this.

One might compare this problem to collecting different types of data using different methodologies. One would not necessarily present all forms of data as being equal. Somehow one would have to sort out and weigh what is most important, reliable, relevant. The same holds true for reporting the perspectives and interests of various participants. Ways of sorting out and weighting these data must exist.

Guiding Principles

Most of these ethical fallacies have at their root the value-free doctrine, which amounts to the evaluator's not taking responsibility for ethical and moral judgments but rather substituting the values of clients, the powerful, or participants as the basis for the evaluation, or by ignoring the issue altogether through seeking refuge in methodology or the contract. These positions are not ethically defensible.

To what degree do the new *Guiding Principles for Evaluators* address such problems? First, the stated assumptions underlying development of the principles are consistent with open and continued refinement; the principles are supposed to begin a dialogue, not end it. The authors also recognize that the principles are relevant for the United States but that they may not work well in other settings. This stance does not entail cultural relativism but simply recognizes (correctly) that settings differ considerably from country to country.

Principles III.A and III.B ("Systematic Inquiry: Evaluators conduct systematic, data-based inquires about whatever is being evaluated"; "Competence: Evaluators provide competent performance to stakeholders") deal with methodological issues. Evaluators should systematically collect data—one can't just walk in and make an assessment off the top of one's head. Also, evaluators should be able to handle these data collection techniques competently.

The authors leave unstated what these techniques should be, thus (wisely) avoiding the ubiquitous quantitative-qualitative dispute. However, the principles assert that there are levels of performance which are unacceptable, and that there should be technical standards within methods by which evaluations can be judged. This is the correct position. In my view, qualitative methods are more deficient in this regard than quantitative ones, which have had years to develop through critical reflection. The same aspiration should be held for qualitative studies.

There is no mention of the methodological fallacy, the idea that methods alone competently executed can and will solve ethical problems. However, the fact that the methodology principles are only two of five major principles indicates that the authors do not believe that methodology solves all problems. Otherwise, the other principles would not be necessary.

Principle III.C ("Integrity/Honesty: Evaluators ensure the honesty and integrity of the entire evaluation process") says somewhat more than that evaluators should not be dishonest. It puts the burden of managing a conscientious process on the evaluator. The evaluator must educate clients and stakeholders and take actions that prevent them from being misled or misinformed. And this includes protecting against conflicts of interests of the evaluator. This admirably rigorous principle will not be easy to live up to.

Principle III.D ("Respect for People: Evaluators respect the security and self-worth of the respondents, program participants, clients, and other stakeholders with whom they interact") carries into the ethics of human research guidelines in place at most universities (Howe and Dougherty, 1994). Not doing injury to participants and informed consent (again the contractual concept) are cautions. However, the authors realize that evaluation by its nature may damage stakeholder interests, though this is (correctly) separated from injury to dignity and self-worth, the later being unnecessary. Of course, one can find borderline cases, but there are many clear-cut examples of correct and incorrect disclosure.

Concern about cultural differences is contained in III.D.5 ("Evaluators have the responsibility to identify and respect differences among participants, such as differences in their culture, religion, gender, disability, age, sexual orientation, and ethnicity"). This introduces the notion of cultural difference but does not deal with the fallacy of relativism. I expect the relativism issue to become a problem as evaluators try to incorporate diverse views. (For one rationale for dealing with multiculturalism, see chapter 10, "Evaluation in Multicultural Societies," House, 1993).

The Public Interest

The most difficult and controversial principle is III.E ("Responsibilities for General and Public Welfare: Evaluators articulate and take into account the diversity of interests and values that may be related to the general and public welfare"). For reasons enunciated earlier, evaluators become nervous when approaching issues of the general public welfare. The authors are to be congratulated for their courage in taking a stand on this issue when they probably could have evaded it; of course, the principles would have been much less valuable without it.

A few things are worth noting about this principle. First, it recognizes that there are "interests" at issue. Evaluators should serve the interests not only of the sponsor but of the larger society, and of various groups within society, particularly those most affected by the program under review. Hence, as a social practice, evaluation entails an inescapable ethic of public responsibility that extends beyond the immediate client. Social justice concerns the manner in which various interests are served, and by interests I mean those things conducive to the achievement of individuals' wants, needs, or purposes, needs being anything necessary to the survival or well-being of individuals. To be free is to know one's interests, to possess the ability and resources, that is, power and opportunity, to act towards them, and to be disposed to do so. Recognizing that there are interests to be served ties evaluation to the larger society and to issues of social justice.

Second, this principle recognizes that there are many diverse interests and values. One mistake of early evaluation was assuming that there were not distinct interests. An issue not addressed is whether the interests to be represented in the evaluation must be voiced by a particular reference group. If one answers "yes" then evaluators will attend to the interests of the powerful because it is they who have the most say in both the evaluation and program most of the time. If one answers "no" then the evaluator is under some obligation to represent the interests of those whose interests are affected by the program and evaluation but who are not present to voice their concerns. This issue distinguishes the pluralist/elitist position from a more egalitarian stance. I believe the evaluator should be concerned about interests not represented.

Furthermore, there is a public interest that is not synonymous with individual or group interests (III.E.5). In other words, there is a public interest that transcends separate interests on some occasions, though this public interest and how it can be served is not specified. Although the evaluator is urged to attend to client interests, these are not to be fulfilled to the exclusion of other interests or the public interest. Hence, the authors avoid the clientism fallacy explicitly (III.E.4) and by implication also the contractual fallacy, though that is unstated.

How the pubic interest is to be defined further is left open. I believe the authors have stretched the limits of consensus of the evaluation community about as far as is possible currently. There seems to be agreement, as represented by these principles, that there are diverse interests, that these should be represented in evaluations, and that there is a general public interest that must take precedence on occasion. This conforms to our notion of pluralist democracy. How these interests should be balanced and weighted requires further debate, discussion, and elaboration of a theory of democracy and social justice.

References

Conner, R. F. "Ethical Issues in the Use of Control Groups." In R. Perloff and E. Perloff (eds.), *Values, Ethics, and Standards in Evaluation*. New Directions for Program Evaluation, no. 7. San Francisco: Jossey-Bass, 1980.

Evaluation Research Society Standards Committee. *Evaluation Research Society Standards for Program Evaluation*. New Directions for Program Evaluation, no. 15. San Francisco: Jossey-Bass, 1982.

Halberstam, D. *The Fifties*. New York: Villard, 1993.

House, E. R. *Professional Evaluation: Social Impact and Political Consequences*. Newbury Park, Calif.: Sage, 1993.

House, E. R., and Care, N. "Fair Evaluation Agreement." *Educational Theory*, 1979, 29, 159–169.

Howe, K., and Dougherty, K. "Ethics, IRB's, and the Changing Face of Educational Research." *Educational Researcher*, 1994, 22 (9), 16–21.

Joint Committee on Standards for Educational Evaluation. *Standards for Evaluations of Educational Programs, Projects, and Materials*. New York: McGraw-Hill, 1981.

Joint Committee on Standards for Educational Evaluation. *Personnel Evaluation Standards*. Newbury Park, Calif.: Sage, 1988.

Joint Committee on Standards for Educational Evaluation. *The Program Evaluation Standards*. (2nd ed.) Newbury Park, Calif.: Sage, 1994.

Ross, D. *The Origins of American Social Science*. Cambridge, U.K.: University of Cambridge Press, 1991.

Sieber, J. E. "Being Ethical? Professional and Personal Decisions in Program Evaluation." In R. Perloff and E. Perloff (eds.), *Values, Ethics, and Standards in Evaluation*. New Directions for Program Evaluation, no. 7. San Francisco: Jossey-Bass, 1980.

Sieber, J. E. (ed.). *The Ethics of Social Research*. 2 vols. Heidelberg, Germany: Springer-Verlag, 1982.

Stufflebeam, D. L. "Professional Standards and Ethics for Evaluators." In M. W. McLaughlin and D. C. Phillips (eds.), *Evaluation and Education: At Quarter Century*. Chicago: University of Chicago Press, 1991, 249–282.

ERNEST R. HOUSE is professor of education at the University of Colorado at Boulder.

Comparing the American Evaluation Association Guiding Principles with other sets of evaluation standards, this chapter addresses reactions to the principles and concludes with recommendations for their use.

A Twenty-Year Veteran's Reflections on the *Guiding Principles for Evaluators*

Robert W. Covert

As the title indicates, the purpose of this chapter is to share my reflections on the newly adopted American Evaluation Association *Guiding Principles for Evaluators*. To do this, it is first important that you understand my background and the perspective that I bring to these reflections. With this framework in mind, I will review three other sets of standards for evaluation that have been used in guiding our practice and will use this analysis as a basis for my argument that, in the profession, our emphasis has broadened from a relatively narrow technical focus to a broader perspective that includes more emphasis on the social human nature of our endeavors. Following this analysis, and in a somewhat different vein, are the results of my asking a colleague to have the graduate students in his evaluation design course react to the principles from their perspectives. I have selected some of their quotes to illustrate their reactions. Their responses will portray a view of how newcomers to our profession view these principles. The final section of the chapter includes some general conclusions and recommendations for the use of the principles.

Personal Background

My formal evaluation career began in 1972 when I took a job with the late Mal Provus at the Evaluation Research Center located in the Education School at the University of Virginia. Even before then, I had conducted some action research on school programs in the Philadelphia Public Schools. At that time there were no formal standards or guiding principles for people conducting program evaluation. The standards that guided practice at that time would have been found in the educational or social science research literature. Since this beginning, I have either conducted, participated in, or supervised over 200 evaluations in a variety of settings, from business to education and human services.

My formal training for evaluation was a Ph.D. in educational psychology from Temple University with a specialization in quantitative research and measurement. My expertise in evaluation was developed on the job during my doctoral program and later as I became involved in a variety of evaluations that were being conducted by the Evaluation Research Center at the University of Virginia where I have been employed for the past twenty-two years. While I was busy conducting evaluations, I also started teaching graduate level courses. First, I taught basic statistics courses; these were followed by the development of a computer data analysis course that taught students how to use statistical data analysis packages. During the time I was teaching the statistics course, I was also teaching an introductory course in program evaluation and assisting my colleague, Bob Brinkerhoff, in training special educators across the country in the Discrepancy Evaluation Model (DEM). As a result of the national evaluation training and my ongoing evaluation project work, I realized the need for a course in instrument construction that emphasized the importance of developing high quality evaluation measures. I subsequently developed a course in instrument construction, which I continue to teach on a yearly basis.

In the early 1980s, I became interested in the qualitative approach to evaluation and, with the help of Jonathan Earl, developed a course in qualitative methods that I still teach annually. As the need for qualitative expertise grew, I developed a second-level course that focuses on advanced qualitative topics and the development of a personal philosophy of inquiry. Subsequently, my teaching interests have expanded to include multicultural education, and I currently teach at least one course per semester in this area. During the summer, I regularly conduct multicultural institutes for teachers and administrators. My evaluation interests, although still very broad, have begun to focus more on the importance of culture and how this affects the work that I do.

I have been an active member of the American Evaluation Association since its inception and served as its second president. I have been a board member and served as the coordinator of membership services since the organization began. Before my involvement in AEA, I was a member of the Evaluation Network (ENet) and attended the first meeting held at Snow Mass, Colorado.

Currently, I am the coordinator for the graduate program in evaluation in the Curry School of Education. I teach courses in evaluation methodology and multicultural education. I advise students, supervise dissertations, direct evaluation projects, and conduct research in multicultural education.

From this perspective I was pleased to be asked to give my reactions to the *Guiding Principles for Evaluators*. As I watched the development of these principles, and saw them change as a result of AEA members' reactions, it struck me that these principles were considerably different from the standards created by the Joint Committee on Standards for Educational Evaluation, the

Evaluation Research Society (ERS) Standards Committee, and the General Accounting Office.

Analysis of Existing Standards

The documentation for the three sets of standards to be analyzed include: *Standards for Evaluation Practice* (Rossi, 1982), which will be referred to as the ERS Standards; *Standards for Evaluation of Educational Programs, Projects, and Materials* (Joint Committee on Standards for Educational Evaluation, 1981), which will be referred to as the Joint Committee Standards; and *Government Auditing Standards* (United States General Accounting Office, 1988 revision), which will be referred to as the GAO Standards. (Although the GAO was formed initially to conduct only financial audits for the legislative branch of the government, it now performs a much broader function, including program evaluation.) The first two sets of standards were selected because they have been most recognized by AEA board members in our continuing discussions of evaluation standards. The GAO Standards were chosen because they reflect a governmental approach to standard setting within an agency that conducts numerous important evaluations. An overview of the three sets of standards is shown in Table 4.1.

The ERS Standards are organized according to the steps in the evaluation process. The fifty-five items take the form of simple admonitory statements and are divided into six different categories: Formulation and Negotiation, Structure and Design, Data Collection and Preparation, Data Analysis and Interpretation, Communication and Disclosure, and Use of Results (Rossi, 1982). The categories with the most emphasis are Formulation and Negotiation and Data Collection and Preparation, with twelve standards each, followed closely by Communication and Disclosure and Data Analysis and Interpretation, with ten and nine standards, respectively. The categories having the fewest standards are Use of Results and Structure and Design, with six standards apiece. In the standard document, the individual standard statements are grouped according to procedural categories and are preceded by a paragraph description of the category. The standard document also includes a chapter description of how standards were developed, along with a series of chapters describing a variety of evaluators' reactions to the standards.

The Joint Committee Standards are organized according to the four important attributes of an evaluation (Joint Committee, 1981) and include a total of thirty individual standards. These four attributes are Utility, Feasibility, Propriety, and Accuracy. The attribute area with the most standards is Accuracy, with eleven, followed by Utility and Propriety, with eight standards each. Feasibility has the fewest standards, three. The Joint Committee document provides the reader with a functional table of contents that includes the following general categories: administering evaluation, analyzing information, budgeting evaluation, deciding whether to evaluate, defining the evaluation problem, designing evaluation, collecting information, contracting evaluation, reporting

Table 4.1. Summary of Evaluation Standards

ERS Standards	Joint Committee Standards	GAO Standards
Formulation and Negotiation	*Utility Standards*	*General Standards*
1. Purposes and characteristics of the program	1. Audience identification	Qualifications
2. Audience, needs and expectations	2. Evaluator credibility	• Proficiency
3. Type, objectives, range of activities for evaluation	3. Information scope and selection	• Continuing professional education
4. Sound, prudent and ethically responsible cost estimate	4. Valuational interpretation	Independence
5. Cost-benefit of evaluative information	5. Report clarity	• Personal impairments
6. Feasibility of the evaluation	6. Report dissemination	• External impairments
7. Restrictions on data access or dissemination	7. Report timeliness	• Organizational independence
8. Conflict of interest	8. Evaluation impact	Due Professional Care
9. Rights and welfare of parties	*Feasibility Standards*	• Planning
10. Technical and financial accountability	1. Practical procedures	• Conducting
11. Formal agreements	2. Political viability	• Reporting
12. Capabilities	3. Cost effectiveness	Quality Control
Structure and Design	*Propriety Standards*	• Internal
13. Approach to evaluation	1. Formal obligation	• External
14. Estimating effects	2. Conflict of interest	*Financial Audits*
15. Sampling methods	3. Full and frank disclosure	Field Work Standards
16. Reliability and validity of measures	4. Public's right to know	• Planning (audit needs, compliance)
17. Appropriateness of procedures and instruments	5. Rights of human subjects	• Evidence (working papers)
18. Cooperation	6. Human interactions	• Internal controls
Data Collection and Preparation	7. Balanced reporting	Reporting Standards
19. Data collection and preparation plan	8. Fiscal responsibility	• Auditing standards
20. Departures from original plan	*Accuracy Standards*	• Compliance
21. Staff competency	1. Object identification	• Internal controls
22. Preservation of human dignity	2. Context analysis	• Financial related
23. Verification of reliability and validity	3. Described purposes and procedures	• Privileged and confidential information
24. Sources of errors	4. Defensible information sources	• Distribution
25. Biased data collection	5. Valid measurement	
26. Minimum disruption	6. Reliability measurement	
27. Risks and informed consent	7. Systematic data control	

28. Unauthorized release
29. Complete documentation
30. Irrecoverable loss of data

Data Analysis and Interpretation

31. Analysis
32. Assumptions and analytic procedures
33. Appropriateness of analysis
34. Unit of analysis
35. Analysis–justification
36. Documentation for replication
37. Statistical and practical significance
38. Rival explanations
39. Findings vs. judgments/opinion

Communication and Disclosure

40. Findings–clarity, fairness and completeness
41. Clarity of language
42. Findings and recommendations
43. Assumptions–general
44. Limitations and need for further study
45. How findings were derived
46. Appropriate feedback
47. Disclosure procedures
48. Authorization for release
49. Organization of documentation

Use of Results

50. Timely dissemination
51. Misinterpretation and misuse
52. Side effects
53. Distinguish findings from recommendations
54. Recommendations–costs/benefits of alternatives
55. Evaluator and advocacy roles

8. Analysis of quantitative information
9. Analysis of qualitative information
10. Justified conclusions
11. Objective reporting

Performance Audits
Field Work Standards
- Planning
- Supervision
- Compliance
- Internal controls
- Evidence

Reporting Standards
- Form
- Timeliness
- Contents
- Presentation
- Distribution

Note: The numbers or lack of numbers is consistent with the way these standards have been portrayed in the source documents.

evaluation, and staffing evaluation. Each of the standards is then stated along with an overview, guidelines, pitfalls, caveats, and illustrative cases. The document includes a statement about how the standards were developed.

The GAO Standards are organized in a different manner from either the ERS or Joint Committee Standards and include considerable emphasis on financial auditing. The thirty-six standards are divided into the three categories of General Standards, Financial Audits, and Performance Audits. Subcategories under the General Standards are qualifications, independence, due professional care, and quality control. Both the Financial Audit and Performance Audit categories are subdivided into field work standards and reporting standards. The major categories initially include a statement of purpose followed by the statement of the individual standards, with a set of explanatory comments for each standard. The document includes an introductory chapter and a chapter describing the different types of government audits.

The new AEA principles are organized around five principles: Systematic Inquiry, Competence, Integrity/Honesty, Respect for People, and Responsibilities for the General and Public Welfare. Each of the principles is stated and followed by a series of explanatory statements. The document includes a description of how the principles were developed and the assumptions underlying their development.

Before reflecting on these different sets of standards and principles, it is important to acknowledge that each set was developed by a different group for a somewhat different purpose and with a different audience in mind. At the same time, each of these documents has influenced and will continue to influence the practice of program evaluation. All reflect an attempt to articulate the principles that make for rigorous evaluations.

One of the most striking features of the AEA principles is their inclusiveness. A review of the language used in past documents reveals implicitly and explicitly that certain evaluation methods and approaches have been given more credibility than others. In particular, quantitative methods are generally assumed, and the language of quantitative approaches is used in the wording of many of the methodological standards. The AEA principles go to great lengths to ensure that both systematic inquiry and competence are not linked to one paradigm or methodology. Instead, they place emphasis on appropriate training and correct applications of the evaluation approach selected for a particular evaluation problem.

Another observation regarding the AEA document is that the emphasis has changed from primarily focusing on methodology and methodological language to the use of a less technical language that is more accessible to a wider audience and places more emphasis on human rights issues. These human rights concerns can be found in both the ERS and Joint Committee Standards, but they are listed as individual standards at the same level as the methodological standards. The GAO document does not directly address these concerns and places major emphasis on following appropriate procedures and being in compliance with the law. To illustrate the point about language, let us look at the following examples. In the ERS Standards, the Joint Committee Standards, and the GAO Standards, the major categories are all named with labels relating to methodology (for example, Formulation and Negotiation, Feasibility, Communication and Disclosure, Field Work, Accuracy, Compliance, and Reporting). In the new principles, the labels Integrity/Honesty, Respect for People, and Responsibilities for General and Public Welfare are illustrative of the different language that accentuates the general human rights concerns. This alternative language and new emphasis provide a fresh focus for the evaluation profession. It is expansive in at least two ways. First, it places more emphasis on the importance of respecting the program participants as a major area of concern for all evaluators by making Respect for People one of the five principles. Second, it explicitly highlights the responsibility of the evaluator to maintain integrity and honesty of the evaluation throughout the process. Both of these concerns have been addressed in the other documents, but the AEA task force has reemphasized them by making them a major focus of the Guiding Principles.

Another new emphasis found in the AEA principles relates to the fifth principle: Responsibilities for General and Public Welfare. Both the ERS and Joint Committee Standards have individual standards alluding to aspects of this dimension of evaluation, but the emphasis has previously been missing. For example, in the ERS Standards the second standard listed under Formulation and Negotiation is, "The clients, decision makers, and potential users of the evaluation results should be identified and their information needs and expectations be made clear. Where appropriate, evaluators should also help identify areas of public interest in the program." Another example from the ERS standards is Standard 54, which reads: "In making recommendations about corrective action, evaluators should carefully consider and indicate what is known about probable effectiveness and costs of the recommended courses of action." Another type of example that is included in the Joint Committee Standards deals with political viability. This standard, categorized under Feasibility, reads: "The evaluation should be planned and conducted with the anticipation of the different positions of various interest groups, so that their cooperation may be obtained, and so that possible attempts by any of these groups to curtail evaluation operations or to bias or misapply the results can be averted and counteracted." Each of these examples suggests important aspects of this responsibility, but at the same time their importance is diminished in light of the numerous other standards to be considered. There are other standards within the other documents that allude to this issue, but by making Responsibilities for General and Public Welfare one of five principles at the same level as Systematic Inquiry and Competence, the AEA task force sets an important new precedent. It says that we are not only concerned that our profession be rigorous and well prepared, but that we are also concerned about the public welfare. For many of us who have been practicing evaluation for a long time, this helps to reaffirm our commitment to being change agents and validates our reasons for being evaluators. In other words, we chose to be evaluators so that we could contribute to making the world a better place.

Student Perspectives

This section of the chapter will address the AEA principles document specifically, integrating my comments with selected reactions from twenty-two graduate students enrolled in a graduate-level course on evaluation design. The students wrote from one to four pages in response to an assignment to write their reactions to the AEA Guiding Principles. As you might expect, the responses were extremely varied. In general, about one third of the students were positive and supportive of the principles, another third were fairly negative about the document, and the other third were difficult to classify, either because they did not give a general reaction or their responses were a combination of both positive and negative reactions. Some of the negative responses criticized the principles as providing little guidance or being incredibly vague and close to worthless. One student's response was: "This document seems like a lot of big words on official looking paper and most likely represents a large monetary expenditure. Yes, it most definitely qualifies as an American 'something Association.'" On the positive side were comments that the principles seem a reasonable approach and should help to unify and strengthen the association. One student commented, "As an evaluator, the principles would assist me in providing a quality evaluation. By following the principles or at least considering each of them when deciding whether or not to take on a client or during the process of evaluation, this would help me to focus my decision making. I am glad to see that someone has taken on this much-needed endeavor. Even in this draft form, I intend to review these principles as I carry out two evaluation plans." These very diverse reactions provide us as evaluators with important information for deciding how to use these principles, both in terms of training people to be evaluators and in informing people outside our profession what we are about. One way to acknowledge and incorporate this diversity of perspective into revisions of these principles is to include a broader representation in a working group that could be formed to regularly review the document. This is especially true if our purpose is to use the principles with a wider audience than just AEA members. This broader representation might include graduate students, beginning evaluators, and other stakeholders (for example, clients, program participants, administrators).

Half of the students who wrote reactions to the principles addressed the assumptions portion of the document. In general, they indicated that the assumptions are informative and provided important background knowledge for their understanding. From my perspective, one of the most important assumptions stated is the acknowledgement that these principles have been developed in the context of Western culture. We should recognize the existence of cultural differences within the United States. As we move into the twenty-first century, these cultural values are going to play a more important role in our continuing discussion of guiding principles.

The statement of assumptions in the document is another feature that distinguishes the AEA Guiding Principles from the other standards presentations. The assumptions ground the principles in a larger context of values and philosophy. They are extremely important and should also be regularly reviewed along with the principles in the revision process.

It is noteworthy that the first principle introduced in the text is Systematic Inquiry. The underlying concept of this principle has been the primary focus of the other three sets of evaluation standards. Placing this principle first sends a loud and clear message to the profession and the general public about the importance of rigorous methodology. A major strength of the wording of this principle is that it reflects an appropriate recognition of the diversity of paradigms that can be applied to the evaluation pursuit. The language used in this section is the generic language of inquiry and provides a solid basis for AEA's continuing dialogue about suitable methodology.

One of the problems that the students expressed about the Systematic Inquiry principle was the lack of specific criteria for rigorous evaluations. Although I understand their concern, I agree with the approach taken by the task force in wording this principle. Because the issue of methodological criteria has been addressed in previous sets of standards and numerous textbooks, the reader can be referred to those other sources, which reflect the wide variety of methods and approaches that are available to the professional evaluator.

Competence, the second principle, puts the focus of the document clearly on the evaluator and the skills and experiences that he or she needs to undertake an evaluation. This issue elicited the most concern from the graduate students. The problem was addressed in one way or another by half of the respondents. The students had two general reactions to this principle. Their first was that there was not enough specification, and their second concerned the implications of this principle for evaluator certification. In the past, the different sets of standards have addressed this competence issue by putting their emphasis on the evaluation itself and then including a standard or two about evaluator competency. The significance of the Competence statement in the new AEA document is that it has the added emphasis of being one of five guiding principles. At the same time it is vague about what competence means. I think that it is time for the AEA board to begin to address the issue of evaluator competence and its implication for certification or licensure. One possible extension of this work would be to engage a new task force with a strong representation from the Teaching Evaluation Topical Interest Group to confront this issue.

One student reaction to the Integrity/Honesty principle was, "Some would regard this as a given and therefore find it unnecessary to mention." I agree with the student that many would regard honesty as a given; at the same time I think there is considerable value in stating this principle explicitly because it says a lot about our basic values as a profession. One of my observations about this principle is that the focus of both the statement of the principle and the accompanying comments is on the honesty and integrity of the evaluation process. I would suggest that it is also important to recognize the honesty and integrity of the evaluator.

Conclusions

My 1987 presidential address to AEA discusses the issue of ethics as it relates to the profession of evaluation (Covert, 1988) and makes the point that ethics can be divided into two general domains: using the methodology appropriately and having respect for people. The fourth AEA principle, Respect for People, places important emphasis on that second domain. In particular, this principle also emphasizes the importance of recognizing and respecting the differences according to culture, religion, gender, disability, age, sexual orientation, and ethnicity. It admonishes evaluators to be mindful of potential implications to these differences in all phases of the evaluation process and to respect the various stakeholders' dignity and self-worth. It suggests that those of us who train evaluators systematically address these complex and sensitive issues in our courses. This new emphasis on multicultural issues and on responsibilities for the general and public welfare makes this principle document a valuable resource to the evaluation professional. By making evaluators accountable to the general public, it brings the profession of evaluation into the larger political context.

Finally, I think one implication of the Guiding Principles document is that it opens up the profession to a more thorough discussion of ethics. Gail Honea, in a series of interviews about ethics with evaluators in the public sector, concludes that ethics were rarely discussed, and when they were, they focused mainly on technical and political issues (Honea, 1992). The inclusion of the latter three principles will hopefully help legitimize a broader discussion of the respect dimension of ethics within the profession.

These principles represent a major step forward in the development of the profession of evaluation. The language of the principles is very inclusive, and as such it also helps to create a language of respect that appreciates the diversity of perspectives within AEA. The document should be widely circulated. It should serve as the content basis for a task force on evaluator competency and certification. It should be critically reviewed by different groups of stakeholders to determine their understandings of its content. A regular revision process should be designed and implemented. The use of the principles should be studied and the results shared with the organization and those responsible for keeping the document updated. A study that systematically links the principles to other standard documents and research competencies needs to be conducted and published.

In conclusion, I strongly support the *Guiding Principles for Evaluators*. I will use these principles not only to guide my own practice but also in my teaching. I commend the AEA members, the AEA board, and particularly the task force for their work. I think that this represents a major step in the growth of our profession.

References

American Evaluation Association. *Guiding Principles for Evaluators*. Charlottesville, Va.: American Evaluation Association, 1994.

Covert, R. W. "Ethics in Evaluation: Beyond the Standards." *Evaluation Practice*, 1988, 9 (1), 32–37.

Honea, G. E. "Ethics and Public Sector Evaluators: Nine Case Studies." Unpublished doctoral dissertation, Department of Educational Studies, University of Virginia, 1992.

Joint Committee on Standards for Educational Evaluation. *Standards for Evaluation of Educational Programs, Projects, and Materials*. New York: McGraw-Hill, 1981.

Rossi, P. H. (ed.). *Standards for Evaluation Practice*. San Francisco: Jossey-Bass, 1982.

United States General Accounting Office. *Government Auditing Standards*. Washington, D.C.: U.S. Government Printing Office, 1988.

ROBERT W. COVERT *is associate professor at the Curry School of Education, University of Virginia. He coordinates the masters and doctoral programs in educational evaluation.*

The American Evaluation Association Guiding Principles and the Joint Committee Program Evaluation Standards have stated intentions that sound alike, but are they? This analysis leads to the conclusion that they are different in important ways.

Standards and Principles

James R. Sanders

The question of overlap between the American Evaluation Association *Guiding Principles for Evaluators* (1994) and the standards published by the Joint Committee on Standards for Educational Evaluation (*Personnel Evaluation Standards*, 1988; *Program Evaluation Standards*, 1994) has been raised. Why do evaluators need two documents to guide their professional practices? Is this a sign of standards proliferation? After all, the American Psychological Association (APA) has a Code of Ethics. The National Council on Measurement in Education (NCME) has a Code of Fair Testing Practices. These organizations and the American Educational Research Association (AERA) have the AERA/APA/NCME Standards for Educational and Psychological Testing. The purpose of this chapter is to provide one response to these questions and to invite comment. A healthy professional dialogue can be productive if new issues or insights emerge from the discussion.

Background

The AEA Guiding Principles were developed in 1993–1994 by a task force of four AEA members (Dianne Newman, Mary Ann Scheirer, William Shadish, chair, and Christopher Wye). This task force was created by the AEA board to develop general guiding principles rather than specific standards of practice.

The Joint Committee on Standards for Educational Evaluation was created in 1975 as a spinoff of the AERA/APA/NCME test standards committee. Its charge was to develop standards for educational evaluation generally, not just for using tests in evaluation. It published the *Standards for Evaluations of Educational Programs, Projects, and Materials* (1981), *Personnel Evaluation Standards* (1988), and *Program Evaluation Standards* (1994). There are fifteen sponsoring organizations of the Joint Committee, including AEA and the founding three, AERA, APA, and NCME. The Joint Committee became a continuing, self-standing body in 1981, and its operating procedures (Sanders, 1994) were accredited by the American National Standards Institute (ANSI) in 1989. Standards approved by ANSI become American National Standards. The Joint Committee *Program Evaluation Standards* were approved by ANSI in 1994.

Comparison of the AEA Guiding Principles and Joint Committee Standards

At first glance when comparing the AEA *Guiding Principles for Evaluators* and the Joint Committee *Program Evaluation Standards*, some obvious differences appear between the two documents. The five principles take up a six-page document. The thirty standards take up a 222-page book. A closer inspection, however, reveals that the five AEA principles are accompanied by twenty-three normative statements to guide evaluation practice. The Joint Committee standards are also normative statements to guide evaluation practice, and each is tied to one of four attributes of sound program evaluation: utility, feasibility, propriety, and accuracy.

The AEA principles are intended to be general guiding principles, rather than specific standards of practice. The intention of the task force was stated to be "to articulate a set of principles that should guide the professional practice of evaluators, and that should inform evaluation clients and the general public about the principles they can expect to be upheld by professional evaluators" (American Evaluation Association, 1994, p. 2).

The Joint Committee standards are intended to be principles "that, if met, will enhance the quality and fairness of [the] professional practice [of] evaluation" (1994, p. 2). "The Standards are an effort to provide guidance to effective evaluation" (1994, p. xviii). Intended audiences are "people who commission evaluations, conduct evaluations, and/or who use the results of evaluation" (1994, p. 4).

Certainly some striking differences and similarities exist. The differences in document size can be attributed to the support material provided for each standard by the Joint Committee: overviews with clarification, guidelines, and common errors collected from the field, illustrative cases showing how the standard may be violated and achieved, and supporting documentation for the standard. The similarities in intent do raise questions about whether there is also similarity in substance.

The analysis provided in Table 5.1 is an attempt to look at similarity in substance between the two documents. Having done the analysis, I can safely say that there are no conflicts or inconsistencies between the two. Although there may be some minor disagreement about where AEA statements should be placed within the framework of the Joint Committee standards, the overall advice is very consistent, with both documents strongly emphasizing accuracy of results, inclusion of stakeholders in the evaluation process, regard for the welfare of evaluation participants, and a concern for service to stakeholders, the community, and society.

Some AEA normative statements are broad and general (that is, III.A.1, III.D.5, III.E.1). One principle is specific and focused (III.B, Competence). The AEA Guiding Principles do not get into methodology and procedures, as is evident from Table 5.1. They do highlight appropriate professional behaviors of evaluators. As one would expect, the greatest overlap is between the Joint Committee propriety standards and the AEA principles III.C, III.D, and III.E.

One area covered by the AEA Guiding Principles is not dealt with explicitly in the Joint Committee Standards. AEA normative statement III.B.3 asserts that evaluators should continually seek to maintain and improve their competencies. This is good professional advice that does not apply directly to a particular evaluation study.

Questions and Answers

The questions posed at the beginning of this commentary deserve some discussion. I will provide a response here but invite further open discussion in forums such as AEA's annual meeting, *Evaluation Practice*, or AEA's new electronic networking offerings.

Why Do Evaluators Need Two Documents to Guide Their Professional Practices? AEA normative statement III.B.3 provides one clue about a difference between these two documents. Some expectations for professionals do not apply to any one specific study. Instead they are part of an expected professional lifestyle: lifelong learning in the case of III.B.3. The AEA principles promote a lifestyle of systematic inquiry, professional development, honesty, respect, and concern for society. These are characteristics expected in all that we do as professionals. They permeate day-to-day activities. In this way the documents are different because the focus of the Joint Committee standards is on the particular (evaluation) and its soundness. Both documents provide important guidance for the evaluation community.

Why Not Merge the Documents? The overlap shown in Table 5.1 reflects consistency, not redundancy. There are no disagreements, but each document provides guidance for different aspects of professional behavior: AEA principles for professional values and Joint Committee standards for professional performance. AEA has provided leadership to the evaluation community through its role as developer of the principles and collaborator on the Joint Committee standards. The documents serve different purposes and, consequently, should remain separate.

Is This Standards Proliferation? One of the characteristics of a profession is that it has its own self-imposed standards that are accepted by members of the profession. Scriven (1993) has described evaluation as a transdisciplinary profession, and there is a danger that discipline-based evaluators, probably

Table 5.1. A Comparison of the AEA Guiding Principles and the Joint Committee Program Evaluation Standards

			A. Systematic Inquiry	B. Competence	C. Integrity/ Honesty	D. Respect for People	E. Responsibilities for General and Public Welfare
Utility	U1	Audience Identification				D-5	E-1
	U2	Evaluator Credibility		B-1, B-2		D-5	E-1
	U3	Information Scope and Selection	A-2			D-5	E-1
	U4	Valuational Interpretation				D-5	E-1, E-5
	U5	Report Clarity				D-5	E-1, E-2, E-3
	U6	Report Dissemination				D-5	E-1, E-3
	U7	Evaluation Impact				D-5	E-1
Feasibility	F1	Practical Procedures					
	F2	Political Viability			C-3, C-6	D-5	E-1, E-4
	F3	Cost Effectiveness				D-4	
Propriety	P1	Service Orientation				D-5	E-1, E-4, E-5
	P2	Formal Obligations			C-2, C-6		E-4
	P3	Rights of Human Subjects				D-1, D-5	E-1
	P4	Human Interactions				D-2, D-3, D-5	E-1
	P5	Full and Fair Reporting			C-1	D-5	E-1, E-4
	P6	Disclosure of Findings			C-5	D-2, D-3, D-5	E-1, E-4
	P7	Conflict of Interest			C-3, C-4	D-5	E-1, E-4
	P8	Fiscal Responsibility			C-1, C-7		

		A. Systematic Inquiry	B. Competence	C. Integrity/ Honesty	D. Respect for People	E. Responsibilities for General and Public Welfare
Accuracy	A1 Object Identification					
	A2 Context Analysis	A-3				
	A3 Described Purposes and Procedures	A-2, A-3				
	A4 Defensible Information Sources	A-2				
	A5 Valid Measurement	A-1		C-6		
	A6 Reliable Measurement	A-1				
	A7 Systematic Data Control	A-1				
	A8 Analysis of Quantitative Information	A-1				
	A9 Analysis of Qualitative Information	A-1				
	A10 Justified Conclusions	A-3		C-6		E-2
	A11 Objective Reporting			C-5	D-5	E-1, E-4
	A12 Metaevaluation	A-1-3	B-1-2	C-1-5	D-1-5	E-1-4

Note: The entries in the cells are the normative statements associated with each AEA Guiding Pinciple.

because they are not members of AEA, may not be aware of applicable standards developed outside of their primary professional organization. In such cases, new and redundant standard setting projects may be undertaken. Standards proliferation currently does not seem to be a problem. AEA has an important role to play in communicating its standards and guiding principles to an increasingly multidisciplinary membership who can then inform their discipline-based colleagues of their existence.

Conclusion

Stufflebeam (1991) discussed the relationship between the Joint Committee standards and ethical issues in evaluation and concluded that the standards provided some guidance to evaluators for dealing with ethical issues, but that the issues were complex, not well understood, and not well documented. The AEA principles move the profession of evaluation ahead by bringing to the attention of its members certain expectations of professional behavior. By identifying and stating professional values, the AEA *Guiding Principles for Evaluators* do contribute to the socialization of members of the evaluation profession.

References

American Evaluation Association. *Guiding Principles for Evaluators*. Charlottesville, Va.: American Evaluation Association, 1994.

Joint Committee on Standards for Educational Evaluation. *Personnel Evaluation Standards*. Newbury Park, Calif.: Sage, 1988.

Joint Committee on Standards for Educational Evaluation. *Program Evaluation Standards*. Newbury Park, Calif.: Sage, 1994.

Sanders, J. R. "The Process of Developing National Standards That Meet ANSI Guidelines." *Journal of Experimental Education*, 1994, 63, 5–12.

Scriven, M. *Hard-Won Lessons in Program Evaluation*. New Directions for Program Evaluation, no. 58. San Francisco: Jossey-Bass, 1993.

Stufflebeam, D. L. "Professional Standards and Ethics for Evaluators." In M. W. McLaughlin and D. C. Phillips (eds.), *Evaluation and Education: At Quarter Century*. Ninetieth Yearbook of the National Society for the Study of Education, Part 2. Chicago: University of Chicago Press, 1991.

JAMES R. SANDERS is professor of education and associate director of the Evaluation Center, Western Michigan University. He currently serves as chair of the Joint Committee on Standards for Educational Evaluation.

As useful as they are, the American Evaluation Association Guiding Principles fail to appreciate the precarious position of the evaluator who speaks truth to power, and their near total focus on elaborating further responsibilities for the evaluator may increase the evaluator's vulnerability to partisan attack.

Comments on the Guiding Principles

Eleanor Chelimsky

The development of professional standards and guiding principles typically signals the increasing maturity of a field and, as such, is a welcome and happy event in evaluation. On reading through the new AEA *Guiding Principles for Evaluators* in January, 1994, I was greatly impressed with the quality of the work that had been done, with the effort made to be inclusive of the varying emphases and values held by the many different strands of our profession, and with the ideals of integrity, competence, fairness to all, and humility that seem to permeate the document. The five principles are not prioritized, however, and the fear I have is that they may increase the evaluator's current vulnerability to partisan attack rather than reduce it.

The context in which evaluation is most often practiced requires a great deal of courage on the part of the evaluator: to ask and maintain the difficult questions, to perform a valid (unbiased) analysis or synthesis, to report the findings precisely as they emerge from the data and the work performed. At all of these points (and others) in the evaluative process, evaluators are subject to attacks based on fear of what the evaluation will find (or has found) and how it will affect the entities or persons concerned.

In the past, these attacks usually have focused on the methods used in the evaluation, the competence or qualifications of the evaluators, and their objectivity or independence with respect to the issue under study. That is because inadequate methodology, dubious skills, and partisanship represent clear and well-recognized threats to the credibility of an evaluation's findings. Efforts to discredit an evaluation based on recognized standards of practice will often follow after pressures on the evaluator—varying from gentle through acute to outright intimidation—have failed.

In setting guidelines for evaluators, therefore, it seems important to recognize these realities of the evaluative environment, first by considering ways to nurture and protect the evaluator's ability and willingness to stand up for what the data show and what he or she believes to be the truth, and second by avoiding the introduction of further responsibilities that could inadvertently provide new bases for attacks seeking to invalidate or neutralize an evaluation's findings for partisan purposes.

My sense, therefore, is that the current Guiding Principles need:

Prioritization. (Telling the truth to people who may not want to hear it is, after all, the chief purpose of evaluation.)
More emphasis on the importance of the evaluator's independence and insulation from pressure.
More attention to the ways in which guiding principles could be used to discredit a methodologically strong, objective, and important evaluation.
More prudence about adding new burdens to the considerable load already being borne by the evaluator.

Speaking truth to power is a risky and often painful task, but that is what the evaluator has to do and the Guiding Principles should try to strengthen his or her hand in doing so. Reading the current document, I come away with the feeling that we have been most attentive to the warts and failings of evaluators but not sufficiently so to the difficulties inherent in the evaluation environment. It is true that the shortcomings of evaluators are real and important to address; however, in my experience, the chief barrier to producing useful evaluations lies not in the evaluator but in the evaluation milieu, which may or may not allow the evaluator to be truthful about the merits of the program or policy that has been evaluated.

ELEANOR CHELIMSKY *is former director of the Program Evaluation and Methodology Division of the United States General Accounting Office.*

Judging the American Evaluation Association principles to be weak statements, difficult to apply in concrete circumstances, and potentially misleading through ambiguity, the author argues for more concern with doing good research rather than getting everyone's approval.

Doing Good and Getting It Right

Peter H. Rossi

It is almost customary for professional associations to have some written code describing what is proper and what is improper conduct in the pursuit of the relevant professional activity. Such a written code appears most frequently if the profession in question includes members who do applied work. Professionals who work for fees paid by clients may need the *bona fide* that both association membership and a written professional code appear to provide, and that need may be the stimulus for associations to adopt such statements.

Variously called ethical codes, guidelines, or standards, these are typically statements of general principles to be observed in the conduct of the profession involved. Some are strongly worded, almost majestically, in thundering commandments that proscribe and prescribe, backed by quasi-judicial bodies that can consider accusations of violations brought against members and wield sanctions against malefactors. Some professional associations go to the extreme of certification, examining members for competence and certifying their fitness to be professionals. Other codes are weak, laying out general principles that ask members of the professional group to "take into account" or make "due allowance for" various exigencies, and they are not backed by any enforcement bodies. Codes vary from being very detailed and encyclopedic in coverage to being relatively general. I venture that strong, detailed codes exist in professional fields in which consensus has been reached over substance and method, and that weak codes flourish in associations in which members are divided on such matters. And, of course, there are professional associations that do not have any written standards or codes. That does not mean there are no ethics in that profession; it may only mean that there is no way the profession can do harm that needs preventing, that the principles of professional conduct are so obvious that they do not need explicit statement, or that the profession is so divided on the issue of what is proper professional conduct that no given set could achieve sufficient endorsement. In some areas, mainly academic disciplines, most instances of professional misconduct are covered by university regulations. For example, no academic discipline needs a code specifying that plagiarism is unethical because the scientific misconduct rules existing in most universities cover that issue fairly well. If the professional association of an academic discipline does have plagiarism standards, that may simply add emphasis.

The Guiding Principles proposed for the AEA are clearly weak codes. They avoid strong prescriptions and proscriptions and, rather, urge members in a mild tone to observe some fairly vaguely worded principles of conduct. Perhaps that is as it should be for the American Evaluation Association as presently constituted. The membership of the AEA is divided on a number of critical substantive and technical issues. A strongly worded set of standards might easily sunder the weak bonds that bind us together and nullify the compromises that make the AEA possible. Even if proposed, a strongly worded set of standards likely would never get adopted. The AEA task force did the best they could in their effort to produce a set of guiding principles that are acceptable to the AEA leadership and membership.

All that said, weakly stated guiding principles often can be close to no principles at all. Even if each of us practices wildly different evaluation modes, we can all believe in all sincerity that we are acting in accordance with the guiding principles. Are we not, each and all, systematic, competent, honest, respectful, and serving the public welfare?

The main problem with such weak guiding principles is that they are silent on those points on which we often need guidance. For example, the competence principle urges members not to present themselves as competent to do evaluation tasks for which they do not have the appropriate training or experience. Of course, the critical issue is what is competence in evaluation, a topic on which the guiding principle is silent perhaps because the membership is divided. For example, am I competent to take on a contract for an ethnographic process evaluation? I did take some courses in graduate school with Margaret Mead and Ruth Benedict, and I did undertake what would now be called a process evaluation of urban renewal programs in Chicago in the 1950s and used an ethnographic approach. I think I might be able to do a process evaluation again, but there are many AEA members who might think that ethnography has progressed beyond Mead and Benedict and certainly beyond the practices of the 1950s. Analogously, randomized field experiments require skills that go beyond what can be learned in courses in the analysis of experiments, to the point that many statisticians I know would not have the competencies needed successfully to carry out a randomized field experiment. Because the guidelines are silent on what are the appropriate matches between competencies and tasks, the guidelines are not much use to an evaluator and to potential evaluation clients. Of course, it may well be the case that such appropriate matches cannot be specified at present because there is no consensus over what is best practice. If so, then it makes no sense to urge that each evaluator assess whether she or he has the competence to undertake some evaluation task.

The standards also remind evaluators that they should have due regard for the public interest and good. I am for that, as are most, if not all, AEA members. Of course, what is the public good is the bone of contention among political parties, political ideologies, and even world religions. I believe that this principle could be stated less vaguely. For example, this principle would be more meaningful if it flatly stated that evaluators would be serving the public good if they refused to undertake classified evaluation research, or that serving the public good means making evaluation findings available to all stakeholders, professional journals, and the mass media. Analogous specific rules concerning other ways of serving the public interest might also be stated. In general, it would be important to keep in mind that the public interest includes more than just the interests of stakeholders. Along these lines, the statements included under III.E.5 in the proposed guidelines need more emphasis.

I also have some reservations about parts of the draft produced by the committee. In particular some of the principles appear to me to invite misinterpretation. For example, principles III.D.2 and III.D.3 worry me. III.D.2 says that evaluators should seek to maximize the benefits and reduce the harms that might occur from an evaluation. I am in favor of the sentiments that are expressed here, but I would want to make sure just what are the harms and benefits involved. To evaluate, as Scriven reminds us, is to make judgments, and sometimes those judgments can be negative and possibly harmful. For example, my current work in child welfare is going to have results that will be devastating (I think) to child protective service agencies. Is that a harm that I should avoid? There is no way I can avoid that harm without suppressing my findings. Should I do that? The point is that to apply this guiding principle in practice we need more detailed guidance on how to balance harms and benefits. Even a few specific illustrative examples would help.

III.D.4 has a sentence in it that might pose some dangers to the integrity of comparison or control groups: "When it would not endanger the integrity of the evaluation, program participants should be informed if and how they can receive services without participating in the evaluation." I find it hard to envisage the circumstances under which doing so would not endanger the integrity of an evaluation. Giving out such information to a comparison or control group is the equivalent of shooting oneself in the foot, potentially narrowing the differences between them and treatment groups, correspondingly lowering the power of the evaluation. Except in the case of "clinical trials" in which evaluators are also running programs, I think that evaluators ought to stay out of the service delivery end of programs. Of course, my fears may not be warranted, in which case they could be easily calmed by more detailed elaboration of this principle.

I understand that NIH regulations instruct researchers to inform subjects about treatment alternatives and that the task force was reluctant to urge evaluators to violate that rule. I also favor being law-abiding, but when law and regulations require auto-destruction, we should be bold and courageous enough to challenge such strictures. Social scientists have been up to the challenge in standing up for confidentiality of individuals' research protocols to the point that some courts are beginning to respect the view that information gathered from people under the promise of confidentiality is to be regarded as such in the courts.

Principle III.D.5 is now becoming a familiar codicil in a wide variety of documents. It admonishes evaluators to "identify and respect potential differences among participants, such as differences in their culture, religion, disability, age, sexual orientation, and ethnicity." I am in favor of evaluators being aware of these major social groupings, but then the next sentence says that we should be "mindful of the potential implications of these differences when planning, conducting, analyzing and reporting . . . evaluations." What does that mean? For example, our social welfare system now has a strong age bias that effectively transfers income from the young to the old. How am I to be properly "mindful" of this bias? Should I suppress that information? Negotiate with the American Association of Retired Persons about how to say it? The point is that the abstract generality of this guiding principle can lead to meaningless ritual statements of compliance that are close to hypocritical.

What I miss in the statement of principles is some concern for the integrity of evaluation outcomes and for the necessity for evaluators to be courageous in stating their findings as clearly and forcefully as may be justified by the validity of their research. In my view, evaluation is not getting along with everybody but getting it right. It is not negotiation for approval but the search for the best approximation to the truth. I had hopes that the guiding principles would affirm that view in very strong terms, but those hopes have been disappointed. Maybe that is too much to expect from the American Evaluation Association as presently constituted.

The vague generality of the guiding principles might be more acceptable to me if I knew that some set of procedures were in place that would eventually generate case law. Because there is no enforcement mechanism that would seek to apply the principles in specific cases, there is no opportunity for case law to develop. A review body that would accept complaints of violations of the guiding principles on the part of members or other bodies could work through the specific meaning of the principles to provide detailed examples of how to apply the principles in practice. The review body could also serve as a moot court arguing hypothetical cases. For example, if a member were uncertain how best to proceed in some given circumstance, the member could submit details of that troubling circumstance to the body for their consideration. Over time the deliberations of a review body could accumulate a corpus of case law that could provide specific guidance to members. I know that it is too much to expect the AEA to put such a review body in place because that would require more consensus on what is evaluation than currently exists. Yet if a professional association is to go beyond piety, it should have the courage to discipline its members and forcefully to state what are its guiding principles in practice.

Guiding principles phrased so generally that all evaluators can endorse have two main virtues. First, they satisfy the expressions of rectitude that roll around pleasantly within our heads and produce the sort of self-satisfied feeling that I used to get when I left the confession booth having dumped my sins on the parish priest. Second, standards have practical uses. Members will be able to claim conformity almost no matter what they do. A copy of the principles hanging, suitably framed, in my office will assure my clients that I have ethical standards. I am certain that I can claim to subscribe to them. I am also certain that if I held very different views of evaluation, I would also be in compliance.

PETER H. ROSSI *is Stuart A. Rice professor emeritus of sociology at the University of Massachusetts at Amherst.*

Demand for program evaluation has led many government agencies to develop in-house evaluation units, and a web of possible conflicts of interest presents internal evaluators with decisions about ethical actions not encountered by an independent evaluator.

Ethics and Internal Evaluators

Robert G. Lovell

Demand for program evaluation has led many government agencies to develop in-house evaluation units. Through familiarity with the agency's policies and information systems, in-house units reduce evaluation costs and startup time. They provide flexibility because priorities can be readily adjusted. They provide analytical assistance for non-evaluation projects. Finally, they provide a source of knowledgeable contract managers when outside evaluations are needed.

However, under this arrangement, evaluators' relationships with those responsible for operating the programs to be evaluated will not end when the final reports are printed. Further, the evaluators' relationships with their clients—their management—will also continue. Finally, their management is ultimately responsible for the operation of the programs evaluated. This chapter explores the web of possible conflicts of interest which present internal evaluators with some decisions about ethical actions not encountered by an independent evaluator. These possible conflicts vary by the source of the evaluation request, arise in clarifying and stating stakeholders' interests, and develop when attempts are made to correct misuse of results. In large-scale welfare reform demonstrations, at least, a major ethical safeguard (obtaining informed consent from all study participants) may not be an option available to the internal evaluator.

Source of the Evaluation Request

Internal evaluations may begin at the direction of the legislative branch, elected executives, appointed executives, superiors who are also civil servants, or at the suggestion of the evaluators themselves. Each of these sources has implications for the evaluations. Requests from legislators, for example, may come as legislation, with specific completion dates and questions to be answered. These requests are intended to obtain information needed for a subsequent budget cycle, often leaving the evaluator less than a year to report. This in turn may severely limit the methodological options available to the evaluator.

Suppose that the time limitation does not allow for study observations over a sufficient time period, for example, to account for a likely seasonal effect. Since the request is a matter of law, the evaluators' managers may be unable to obtain a time frame adjustment. Should the evaluators refuse the assignment, possibly resulting in an even less-informed decision and creating a possible disciplinary problem? Or should the evaluators complete the evaluation, clearly noting the limitations imposed, even though the product will not meet the "highest appropriate technical standards" envisioned in section III.A.1 of the American Evaluation Association *Guiding Principles for Evaluators*? One obvious strategy is to design a satisfactory study that includes a carefully qualified interim report made available at the time requested, but with the recommendation that decision making await the final report. The danger here is that a legislative decision made on the interim report may be contra-indicated by the final report. Is knowingly taking this risk ethical?

Requests for evaluations from management carry several ethical risks caused by the web of apparent conflict of interest. The management requesting the evaluation supervises the evaluator and is responsible for managing the program to be evaluated. Does the evaluator risk damage to his or her career by publishing a critical evaluation? What if the evaluation request violates section III.C.6's stricture against methodology likely to produce a misleading result or section III.D.2's stricture against undue risk or harm?

In resolving this conflict, much depends on the evaluators' managers. In the long run, evaluations done improperly have no validity and will be discounted; the usefulness of the internal evaluation unit will be reduced or ended if its results are not accepted. However, there may be short-term advantages to political officials in pressuring evaluators to look only at program aspects likely to be positive, or even to falsify results. If their managers succumb to this temptation, evaluators must act. They may attempt to educate their managers, include a dissent in all reports released, refuse to sign the evaluation, refuse the assignment (raising the ethical issues in appealing any resulting disciplinary action), and/or look for new employment. Reference to a clearly stated and widely accepted code of ethics such as the AEA's Guiding Principles may be very helpful in taking any of these actions.

A related question is raised by section III.C.3's emphasis on disclosure. Should each evaluation published by an internal evaluator include an analysis of the degree of conflict of interest involved? Or should this be included only in extraordinary circumstances? A statement of conflict of interest is appropriate when immediate career effects are possible (and the evaluator's management should attempt to prevent this from occurring). Otherwise, I think most evaluation users will assume a low-level conflict of interest caused by general career interests that need not be mentioned.

Pressures to narrow the focus of the evaluation selectively or to falsify results can come from colleagues operating the program to be evaluated. The program managers may not even recognize their overtures as unethical—they may only be seeking morale boosters for their staffs. Here the evaluator needs most to recognize these pressures so that they can be resisted. A discussion of differing professional viewpoints and obligations, including discussion of the AEA Guiding Principles, may be helpful in maintaining personal relationships.

The sum of these pressures apparently led Michael Scriven (1991, p. 198) to conclude that, for the internal evaluator, "Careful management and high quality evaluation can offset the validity handicap, but not the credibility one." I don't subscribe to this dark view of the internal evaluator's chances of being considered credible, at least among those users most likely to apply results directly and to be users of subsequent work. The internal evaluator develops a reputation over time just as any evaluator does. The key point is that this reputation will be lost instantly if he or she succumbs to these pressures, and it may never be regained.

Determination of Stakeholders' Interests

Section III.C.3 requires the evaluator to seek to determine stakeholders' interests in the evaluation and to report them where appropriate. This requirement presents unique problems for public programs. At a minimum, the list of stakeholders includes the legislature which created the program, the executive-branch employees responsible for carrying it out, the population immediately affected by the program, and the taxpayers who pay for it. There will be legislators who voted against the program. The executive branch may be operating the program only because a veto was overridden. Public programs interact in complex and unexpected ways. For instance, a decrease in federal income tax withholding can decrease child support collections for the Aid to Families with Dependent Children (AFDC) program, impacting evaluations of both efforts. Finally, all public programs compete with all others and with all potential programs for scarce resources, making the beneficiaries, real and potential, of other programs stakeholders in the program to be evaluated. How is the evaluator to determine the interests of all of these stakeholders? Strictly interpreted, this requirement seems infeasible for public programs (regardless of the employment status of the evaluator). Sensible limitation is in order. Perhaps the most relevant stakeholders are the program managers and beneficiaries of the program to be evaluated, related or alternative programs, and taxpayers. Their interests should be determined and stated when appropriate.

Correcting Misuse Within Reasonable Limits

Section III.C.5 places an obligation on evaluators to prevent or correct misuse of their results "within reasonable limits." What are these limits when elected or politically appointed officials misuse results? Certainly, evaluators must raise objections within their management structure. If willful, substantial misrepresentation continues, I believe that the evaluators' obligations depend on the availability of the full report. If the report has been publicly released, confronting these officials is the responsibility of the press and of their political opponents. Similarly, if the study could be obtained under a Freedom of Information Act (FOIA) request, the responsibility is external.

However, if the study has been lawfully suppressed (in the absence of a FOIA or beyond its reach), it would seem to become privileged information under section III.C.5 of the code of ethics of the American Society for Public Administration (ASPA), and a conflict exists. This code instructs public administrators to "Respect and protect the privileged information to which we have access in the course of official duties." I see no general resolution for this dilemma. (Adopting this principle on the job does not attenuate public employees' rights or responsibilities as private citizens to take part in the political process and to speak out for their values.)

Many public administrators belong to ASPA; the number who also belong to AEA is unknown to me but might be interesting. The ASPA code of ethics, published in 1984 after a lengthy and intense internal debate (Chandler, 1983; Nigro and Richardson, 1990), instructs public administrators to (in brief):

1. "Demonstrate the highest standards of personal integrity, truthfulness, honesty, and fortitude"
2. "not realize undue personal gain"
3. "Avoid any interest or activity which is in conflict with conduct of our official duties"
4. "Support, implement, and promote merit employment and programs of affirmative action"
5. "Eliminate all forms of illegal discrimination, fraud, and mismanagement of public funds, and support colleagues if they are in difficulty because of responsible efforts to correct such"
6. "Serve the public with respect, concern, courtesy and responsiveness"
7. "Strive for personal professional excellence and encourage the professional development of our associates and those seeking to enter the field"
8. "Approach our organization with a positive attitude and constructively support open communication, creativity, dedication, and compassion"
9. "Respect and protect the privileged information to which we have access in the course of official duties"
10. "Exercise . . . discretionary authority . . . to promote the public interest"
11. "keep up to date on emerging issues and [work with] competence, fairness, impartiality, efficiency, and effectiveness"
12. "Respect, support, and when necessary, work to improve federal and state constitutions and other laws which define the relationships among public agencies, employees, clients, and the public."

The speed and scope of communications today may make correcting misuse difficult for all evaluators, internal and otherwise. I am a co-principal investigator on the General Assistance Project, a study of the termination of Michigan's General Assistance program (a cash welfare program for childless adults) funded by the Ford Foundation. An interesting but not crucial finding in our February 1993 interim report (Kossoudji, Danziger, and Lovell, 1993, p. 42) was that 17.7 percent of those who lost benefits had worked while receiving General Assistance. The Fall 1993 issue of *Policy Review* included an article by Lawrence W. Reed asserting, based on this finding, that "82 percent had never held a job in their lives" (Reed, 1993, p. 65). If true, this would have been a crucial finding, but it was false; our results had been misinterpreted. The editors of *Policy Review* offered all of us an opportunity to comment on the article, and I attempted to correct the misinterpretation in my response (Lovell, 1994). However, by the time our responses were published, George F. Will had used the incorrect interpretation on *This Week with David Brinkley*, a television show presumably viewed by millions. We did not attempt to contact either the television network or Will; I have never seen them issue a retraction, so requesting one seemed useless. Even if a retraction were broadcast, the viewing audience would have changed between shows. Did I make every reasonable effort to correct the misuse of data?

Informed Consent

Some of the largest and potentially most important evaluations now being conducted in the United States are of states' attempts to reform their welfare programs. These reforms are permitted only when waivers of federal regulations have been obtained. In granting these waivers the Department of Health and Human Services (DHHS) requires a comprehensive evaluation. Except in unusual circumstances, DHHS demands a design with random assignment of study families to old and new policies.

Generally, the evaluation must be completed by independent contractors, but in Michigan and other states, contract development and oversight are the responsibility of internal evaluation units. The choice of whether or not to accede to the clear preference for obtaining informed consent expressed in section III.D.1 is, then, shared by internal evaluators, their managers, and the evaluation contractor.

These studies are large; 18,000 families were involved in Michigan's waiver study in the first year, and this number will easily double before the study is complete. No informed consent was sought in Michigan, nor is it sought in most other states. Three reasons are generally given:

1. The Department of Health and Human Services tells states (when asked) that informed consent is not legally required. This position was most

recently upheld in a suit against California's Assistance Payments Demonstration Project, *Beno v. Shalala*.
2. Many waiver packages are designed to get better results at current costs; average spending per family will be approximately equal under old and new policies. Because the increased benefit of the new policy is only theoretical until the evaluation is completed, participants are not knowingly disadvantaged. Further, most data collection is done through existing administrative data systems and thus places no additional burdens on the families involved.
3. Since every family has a right to know how its benefits were calculated, blind studies of welfare policy are not possible. Informing families of the consequences of a decision to participate would allow them to determine which policy appears most beneficial in their particular circumstances. That is, a family could choose a random chance at one policy (by agreeing to participate) or a certain assignment to the other (by refusing). This self-selection effect might be serious enough to invalidate the study.

The first two reasons are certainly not compelling reasons to avoid informed consent for evaluators trying to act ethically (although managers faced with the cost of obtaining and tracking 36,000 consent forms might find the first reason compelling).

The third reason, however, presents a stark decision: no informed consent or no valid evaluation. So far the decision has been to go forward with evaluations; this decision has support at the presidential level. This is what *is* happening. Is it ethical? Welfare programs are legally voluntary but economically coercive; government entitlement programs largely drive out competition from private charities and thus are monopolies. Welfare families are clearly vulnerable to further coercion to cooperate. In stark terms, families dependent on welfare for their basic needs are subjected to the risk of some harm (reduced benefits or other restrictions) for the greater good (learning how to improve the welfare system).

On the other hand, welfare reform and the existence of an American underclass are serious public policy issues. Despite their many inherent methodological limitations (Wiseman, 1993), state-sponsored experiments may be the best politically feasible way to improve the current welfare system. Again, I don't see a general solution for this dilemma. Perhaps the extent to which reforms are truly cost-neutral provides a guide, because equal costs suggest roughly equal benefits.

My question for AEA as the interpretation of the principles develops is, then, how strongly is the preference for informed consent to be interpreted? When is it permissible to carry out large-scale evaluations, including evaluations utilizing random assignment to competing treatments, without informed consent? Does the "feasible and desirable" clause in III.D.1 allow appropriate flexibility or too much?

Conclusions

With a few exceptions (notably in correcting misuse of results and in obtaining informed consent) the AEA Guiding Principles provide a valuable basis for internal evaluators' ethical questions. They should assist internal evaluators both in making professional decisions and in explaining these decisions to their managers. Finally, they will become more valuable to all evaluators as their intent, implications and consequences are explored.

References

American Society for Public Administration. American Society for Public Administration's Code of Ethics. Printed frequently, for example, *Public Administration Review*, 1994, 54 (4), outside back cover.

Beno et al. v. Shalala, Civ. S-92-2135 (ED CA 1993).

Chandler, R. C. "The Problem of Moral Reasoning in American Public Administration: The Case for a Code of Ethics." *Public Administration Review*, 1983, 43 (1), 32–39.

Chandler, R. C., and Plano, J. C. *The Public Administration Dictionary*. New York: Wiley, 1982.

Kossoudji, S., Danziger, S., and Lovell, R. "Michigan's General Assistance Population." An interim report of the General Assistance Termination Project, 1993. (Available from the authors.)

Lovell, R. "Interpretation of Studies Questioned." *Policy Review*, 1994, 68, 85–86.

Nigro, L. G., and Richardson, W. D. "Between Citizen and Administrator: Administrative Ethics and PAR." *Public Administration Review*, 1990, 50 (6), 623–635.

Reed, L. R. "Michigan's Welfare Abolitionist." *Policy Review*, 1993, 67, 65.

Scriven, M. *Evaluation Thesaurus*. Newbury Park, Calif.: Sage, 1991.

Wiseman, M. "Welfare Reform in the States: The Bush Legacy." *Focus*, 1993, 15 (1), 18–36.

ROBERT G. LOVELL is director of the Staffing and Program Evaluation Division of the Michigan Department of Social Services.

This chapter addresses the concerns that full-time evaluators in private practice have about the uses and value of the American Evaluation Association Guiding Principles.

An Independent Consultant's Perspective on the Guiding Principles

Tara D. Knott

One of the things about which I am most proud is the manner in which the American Evaluation Association conducts itself professionally. AEA attempts to hold down membership costs so that all who wish to join may do so, encourages young evaluators in a variety of ways, and provides modest stipends to evaluators from less-developed and poorer countries to attend AEA conferences. This pervasive sensitivity to morality, justice, and equity is apparent in the development of the guiding principles. AEA leadership and the task force itself are to be commended for their thoughtful, systematic, and inclusive approach to the development of these principles.

Background and Practice Description

Having been in private evaluation practice for over ten years, I have worked with all types of organizations—large and small, for-profit and non-profit. These organizations provide services ranging from the development of museum exhibits to the design of technological interventions to the provision of feeding services. My firm, Evaluation Resources Inc. (ERI), has a permanent full-time staff of three and one half, and relies heavily on productive alliances with evaluator colleagues and various field experts. The size and scope of ERI's practice is probably representative of most small evaluation firms.

ERI's philosophy is that consumer needs and outcomes are the most important consideration in all endeavors. ERI therefore is careful to inform potential clients that, although their expectations of the evaluand will be seriously reviewed and considered, along with those of other stakeholder groups, it is the endeavor's impacts on the consumers that will determine the value of the project. This orientation is mentioned here because ERI believes, as do many other evaluators in private practice, that human beings and their wants, needs, and fears do not change simply because they move from a social context to a business context. That is, the values held by people in one situation hold constant across other situations. Further, ERI believes that evaluation clients and the consumers or target populations are more similar in their basic humanity than they are different. This philosophy permeates ERI's practice and will permeate this discussion of the AEA principles.

Assumptions

Assumption II.D states that the purpose of documenting the principles is "to foster continuing development of the profession of evaluation, and the socialization of its members." In order to further develop the principles, they might be tried out in specific situations that are delineated by the task force, and their usefulness in specific situations could be carefully described and evaluated. For example, how useful would the principles be in guiding the professional behavior of evaluators working in educational situations, or those who are involved in health care delivery, or those involved in organization development? Clearly, the principles could not be tested in every instance or context in which evaluators practice, but it does seem possible to identify those major areas in which most evaluators actually work and to test the principles in those areas. Perhaps a listing of the Topical Interest Groups (TIGs) would be a useful place to start this identification process.

Additionally, during the initial five years of their development, it seems useful to subject the principles in a more systematic way to a real-life test in the various stages of the evaluation process. That is, the principles may guide us well during contract negotiation, when the scope, costs, and nature of the evaluation is decided, but fail to be useful once we move to the actual design and/or implementation of the evaluation. The principles ideally should be useful in all of these evaluation stages.

Evaluators at different levels in their careers may also find the principles of varying usefulness. For example, a novice may find the principles extremely helpful, whereas an experienced evaluator might wish they were less, or more, stringent, descriptive, or prescriptive. Over the next five years, the principles, therefore, might be tested in institutions that train evaluators, in situations in which the evaluator using the principles is simply implementing a more experienced evaluator's design, and by those evaluators who are experienced enough to routinely be responsible for developing the design itself.

Additionally, perhaps, the task force or some similar body could develop several criteria or aspects of use that should be examined in these test situations. For example, ease of use, applicability or relevance, or unnecessary constraint might be considered. These criteria could be useful in actually establishing the value of the principles under certain conditions, to certain stages of evaluation practice, and in certain stages of evaluation planning and implementation.

Assumption II.I states that these principles were developed in the context of Western cultures, particularly the United States, and so may reflect the experiences of that context. The task force is to be commended for recognizing and reporting this timely and important constraint given the plethora of cultures with whom many evaluators routinely work. It would seem useful to have the members of the international TIG assist the task force to broaden the context in which the principles are developed. These AEA evaluators are familiar with the unique contextual aspects and issues involved in conducting international evaluation. Eventually all evaluators should be prepared to participate in such ventures as the global village becomes a reality.

Additionally, there are clearly cultures in the United States and elsewhere that may represent special evaluation considerations. These include the physically and mentally impaired, who may require certain types of sensitivities from evaluators to ensure that their values are upheld.

The Guiding Principles

Systematic Inquiry. Obviously evaluators should conduct systematic, data-based inquiries about the evaluand. However, from my perspective, one issue that might be difficult to actually implement is III.A.1, which asserts that evaluators should "adhere to the highest appropriate technical standards in conducting their work." All of us would agree that this is good practice, but few would agree on exactly what those standards might be. For example, what are the "highest appropriate technical standards" for a mainly qualitative evaluation task such as a structured interview? No doubt we can identify several, such as "fair treatment and concern about the interviewee," which would be readily accepted by all evaluators. However, the principle might be more useful if it gave examples of such technical standards for both quantitative and qualitative studies.

III.A.2 will be useful to independent evaluators because it will provide an excellent opportunity to investigate with clients a variety of questions that they may not have considered and that perhaps should be included. It will also help independent evaluators introduce clients to the different approaches that are available to obtain the best answers to the final evaluation questions agreed to.

The third suggestion under principle III.A.3 is imperative for independent consultants. That is, the client must understand the limitations and assumptions that underlie the evaluation. Often, the identified limitations and conditions help convince the client that certain changes, usually decreasing the scope of the evaluation, are desirable. It would be even more helpful if the "contextually appropriate" ways to discuss the "values, assumptions, theories, methods, results, and analyses that *significantly* affect the interpretation of evaluative findings" were illustrated in several ways.

Competence. The provision of "competent performance" (III.B.2) is of course necessary in private practice to maintain the evaluator's professional integrity as well as to enhance the possibility of repeat contracts from a client. The problem is that clients sometimes do not know what is competent work and what is incompetent. I, like many others, spend a good deal of time educating the client about evaluation, its uses, and its special properties. A problem often ensues, however, when clients confuse competency in evaluation with competency in the content area to be evaluated. This is a frequent problem in my specific practice. For example, a client from the banking industry may prefer to hire another banker to evaluate a new customer service or product. The banker contracted for the evaluation may not have evaluation expertise and, because he or she probably has the same experience and training as does the original banker, may be subject to the "good ole boy" syndrome, wherein a positive evaluation is almost guaranteed. Both of these may work against the provision of a competent evaluation. Evaluation competency is quite different from competency in a specific content area or industry, and this should be clarified for the client if at all possible.

An issue of concern with III.B.2 and III.B.3 is the need for all evaluators, including independent consultants, to stretch their professional armamentaria and competencies by routinely trying new approaches. Although the client should not be subjected to incompetent work, evaluators should occasionally attempt new, unfamiliar evaluation approaches, methods of reporting, and so forth, wherever useful and wherever such a practice would clearly not interfere with providing competent evaluation services. As suggested in III.B.3, the evaluator can attend workshops, read, or otherwise learn new techniques to the best of his or her abilities before any new approach is actually tried. Or as suggested in III.B.1, the evaluator can ensure that a member of the evaluation team has the necessary expertise.

It is important to deviate from one's standard approach in order to stay abreast of innovative developments in our field and, perhaps more importantly, to ensure that the evaluator does not become entirely constrained by, or limited to, a single paradigm.

Integrity/Honesty. Principle III.C.1 suggests that it is useful for independent evaluators to be explicit with clients about tasks to be performed, costs, and limitations because these help determine the scope of the contract. Such explicitness also helps ensure that evaluators and clients are aware of their individual responsibilities regarding the evaluation. In my practice, this clarification of roles and responsibilities is imperative.

It also seems clear that evaluators in all contexts occasionally may have difficulty disclosing the interest of other stakeholders "concerning the conduct and outcomes of an evaluation," as is suggested in III.C.3. Certain stakeholders, for whatever reasons, may not want to identify their specific interests in a project. For example, it is difficult to get representatives from some higher education organizations to specify one of their educational interests as wanting to ensure that they obtain their fair share of students. This is understandable because this interest may be interpreted as their being more concerned about money than with providing good education. Such educators would probably not be comfortable with an evaluator's disclosing this interest to other stakeholder groups involved in the project. Although it may be acceptable, and desirable, to reveal this interest to college executive board members, it would not be acceptable to reveal it to the parents of students involved. Perhaps it would be helpful for the task force to provide examples of what is meant by the term "where appropriate" as it appears in III.C.3.

Respect for People. Principle III.D is difficult to use when a variety of cultures and/or contexts is involved. Respect for people is, however, imperative as a guiding principle for independent evaluators because the evaluator is often external to the evaluand; therefore, the formal requesting and granting of various permissions, such as access to certain respondents, serves to indicate to the client that the evaluator indeed is concerned about privacy and that the entire discipline supports this concern.

In many instances, formal explanations and descriptions of confidentiality procedures are requested in writing before permission is granted to contact any respondent. Often, this is the first opportunity to begin teaching the client about evaluation, its practices, and its uses. This issue, then, is the first one in which the client may become aware that evaluation is different from, say, market research, wherein the concern for people and their privacy does not seem as crucial as it must be to evaluators.

A second issue concerns the evaluator's enforcement of the suggestion implicit in following certain informal consent standards, that is, that participants can withdraw at any time and still receive benefits from the evaluand (III.D.1). Evaluators can present this issue to both client and consumers by including it on any written instruments, but it is doubtful that all consumers will actually believe this is the case. Obviously, evaluators cannot control the behavior or understanding of the client (the person funding or requesting the project) or the evaluand's consumers. However, as a guiding principle, this is an important understanding.

III.D.5 suggests that evaluators should be sensitive to the potential differences that exist in participants in an evaluation. In my practice, certain consumer and/or stakeholder groups only accept information if it is collected with recognized input from a member of their groups. Otherwise, the data are suspect. For example, in some health care situations, it is imperative that a health care professional actually serve on the design team. This person's mere presence and verbal acknowledgment of participation helps ensure that the health care client, especially physicians, will accept and use the results.

Responsibilities for General and Public Welfare. This issue is one about which I have strong opinions. Especially today, when many ventures combine the private and public sectors, it is imperative to recognize that clients (those who request or fund the evaluation) may, or may not, have a serious interest in promoting the common good. Some thought, however, is required simply to define what is meant by the "public" and the "general and public welfare" (III.E). For example, the evaluand may use the telecommunications highway proposed in the United States by the Clinton/Gore administration. This proposed electronic network is intended as an infrastructure to transmit all types of telecommunications (satellite, fiber-optic, copper cable) to various groups of people for various purposes. The highway first will cross the nation and eventually connect with similar networks outside the United States. Typically, a specific aspect or component of the telecommunications highway will be evaluated and was probably created for a certain purpose, such as delivering otherwise unavailable educational services to geographically disparate K–12 schools. However, many other uses for this same aspect or component of the telecommunications network will probably also occur. Who, then, is the "public" in this instance? Is it the people in the community for which the part of the highway being evaluated is being constructed? Is it people in the state? Are all citizens of this country a part of this public? Or must the social impact of the evaluand on several continents be considered? How many different "societies" and "cultures" should be included in the "public" as it is impacted by this endeavor? Might the potentially negative impacts be felt by only particular segments of the public? Does the potential public good outweigh the potential harm done by the evaluand to certain segments of the public? In some cases, it would be difficult to identify those population groups that may be impacted in five or ten years. And although common sense and the resources available for the evaluation will help determine the public for the evaluation results, this issue deserves further thought.

The same problem applies to the consideration of "not only the immediate operations" (III.E.2), but the future potential impacts of the evaluand. It is difficult to determine how far in the future is far enough when considering the impacts of the evaluand. Using telecommunications again, the potential future impacts are largely unknown, even for the immediate future of the next three to five years. This principle's usefulness as a guide could be improved if greater specificity were included.

Finally, evaluation results are sometimes restricted, on the front end, to the client only for a given period of time that is included in the contract. This practice often occurs because the evaluation information is used to gain a competitive edge over others in the same industry. During this period of time, even results that may threaten certain stakeholder groups may not be disclosed. This situation, although clearly undesirable, occurs in private practice. Principle III.E.4 is well taken; however, it would be helpful if some suggestions for handling the situation described above were given. Sometimes stakeholders who may be harmed by the evaluand can be informed of possible negative consequences if this is done verbally in the presence of the client. However, all clients will not agree to this approach and, in these instances, it would be difficult, if not impossible, to follow the guidance provided by the principle.

Conclusion

The AEA principles are well thought out and, in general, useful for evaluators in private practice. With the exception of the foregoing, they will assist, and not constrain, independent evaluation consultants.

TARA D. KNOTT is manager of the consulting firm Evaluation Resources Inc. and has been involved in designing and implementing large-scale, multisite evaluations and in evaluating technological interventions in education, especially distance education.

*A response to the American Evaluation Association Guiding
Principles from the perspective of evaluators working in settings
outside the United States is presented here.*

International Perspectives on the Guiding Principles

Michael Hendricks, Ross F. Conner

The preface to the American Evaluation Association (AEA) *Guiding Principles for Evaluators* (American Evaluation Association, 1994) lists several assumptions upon which the set of principles was developed. One of these assumptions states: "These principles were developed in the context of Western cultures, particularly the United States, and so may reflect the experiences of that context. The relevance of these principles may vary across other cultures, and across subcultures within the United States."

How well do the AEA principles apply to evaluators working in cultures outside the United States? This chapter provides an initial answer to this important question.

There are two main benefits to having viewpoints on the principles from evaluators who work outside the typical evaluation settings in the United States. First, it is through contrasts and comparisons that evaluators are able to assess value and change (Rossi and Freeman, 1993; Cook and Campbell, 1979). The AEA principles were developed with the United States context as the baseline or benchmark. Other cultures can provide valuable comparison bases for examining explicit assumptions and issues, as well as for identifying implicit or unrecognized assumptions and biases.

A second benefit to seeking comments from outside evaluators is that they are not as personally invested in the principles as evaluators based in the United States might be. Apart from the cultural distance, therefore, international evaluators bring an interpersonal distance, which can provide a balancing view (Patton, 1990; Posavac and Carey, 1989). The Guiding Principles were developed, by design, by people intimately familiar with the realities of doing evaluation in the United States. This familiarity allowed the creators to craft guidelines that reflect both what is desirable and what is possible. One risk of familiarity, however, is that the creators might lose sight of other issues. Evaluators working in settings outside the United States can provide the counterbalancing view to this possible risk.

The sections below demonstrate these two benefits. After we describe how we selected international evaluators and solicited their viewpoints, we present excerpts from twelve commentaries. We have organized the comments by general topics in order to assist the reader, but apart from some very minor editing, we allow these evaluators to speak in their own words. By doing this, we believe that the benefits of these outside views are conveyed best. In their own culturally anchored ways, these evaluators provide fresh insights on different aspects of the principles, and we have avoided any filtering of these insights by reprocessing them through a United States lens. We conclude the chapter, however, with our own personal overview of what we believe to be the commentators' main points.

Method

To accomplish our goal of collecting a variety of international perspectives, we contacted evaluators who were working outside the context of the United States. We called upon people we knew and upon others suggested to us. As we assembled our list, we sought evaluators from every part of the world and from developed and developing countries. Our goal was to have approximately twelve commentaries from evaluation colleagues from a variety of settings and countries.

We also included in our list of prospective commentators several U.S. evaluators who, like us, have worked in international settings. We felt that these evaluators could provide a useful and unique perspective because they straddle two or more cultures in their activities. However, we decided to minimize the involvement of commentators within the United States in order to give maximum voice to our commentators outside the United States. In this respect, our current motives and methods are similar to our earlier effort to provide a voice for evaluators outside the United States regarding international innovations in evaluation methodology (Conner and Hendricks, 1989).

Thanks to the generosity of the highly experienced evaluators listed below, we achieved our goal of twelve commentators. Each took time from his or her busy schedule to review the draft principles and to write detailed, thoughtful commentaries for our benefit. Two of our commentators are from India (Singh, Sinha), two from Europe (Bemelmans-Videc, Hjelholt), two from Australia (Sharp, Winston), one from Africa (Rwampororo), one from Canada (Love), and four are U.S.-based evaluators with extensive international and cross-cultural experience (Cooley, Duncan, Ginsberg, Rugh). For their help, and for sharing their unique perspectives with U.S.-based evaluators, we are deeply indebted.

Marie-Louise Bemelmans-Videc is head of the Division for Quality Evaluation, Nederlands Court of Audit, the Hague. A professor of public administration at the Catholic University of Nijmegen and an author and editor of several books and reports on evaluation, she is also one of the co-founders of the European Evaluation Society.

Lawrence S. Cooley is president of Management Systems International, an international consulting firm in Washington, D.C. Over the past twenty years he has consulted in dozens of different countries for a wide variety of multilateral and bilateral donor agencies and for private and non-profit development organizations.

Richard Duncan is an independent program evaluation consultant with extensive experience in international evaluation, particularly in Central and South America. Until recently, he co-chaired the AEA's Topical Interest Group on International and Cross-Cultural Evaluation.

Pauline Ginsberg is on the psychology faculty of Utica College of Syracuse University in Utica, New York. She has extensive experience in cross-cultural evaluation issues and was co-chair of the AEA's Topical Interest Group on International and Cross-Cultural Evaluation.

Gunnar Hjelholt is head of his own institute in applied social psychology in Fjerritslev, Jutland, Denmark. During his long and distinguished career as a social psychologist, he has worked mainly in international settings, particularly as a consultant to UNICEF and as a member of the Indian National Monitoring and Evaluation Group.

Arnold J. Love is an independent program evaluation consultant based in Toronto, Canada, with over twenty years of experience in the evaluation field. A past president of the Canadian Evaluation Society, he specializes in building internal evaluation capacity for public and nonprofit organizations.

Jim Rugh is an independent consultant working on community-based evaluations, with a special interest in cross-cultural issues. Based in Sevierville, Tennessee, he currently co-chairs the AEA's Topical Interest Group on International and Cross-Cultural Evaluation.

Rosern Rwampororo is an agricultural economist and monitoring and evaluation specialist with the U.S. Agency for International Development (USAID) in Kampala, Uganda. Previously with the Agriculture Secretariat of the Central Bank of Uganda, she is responsible for designing, monitoring, and evaluating USAID-funded projects in agriculture and natural resources.

Colin A. Sharp is associate professor, Flinders Institute of Public Policy and Management, Flinders University, Adelaide, South Australia. Current president of the Australasian Evaluation Society, he mainly works in human services management, education, and consulting in the public sector.

Anup K. Singh is assistant professor at the Management Development Institute in Gurgaon, Haryana, India. In addition to his teaching, he does extensive consulting for Indian private sector firms and has written recently on the roles of middle managers, the dynamics of personal change, and strategic human resource management.

Jai B. P. Sinha is professor of social psychology at the A. N. Sinha Institute of Social Studies in Patna, Bihar, India. He is also president of the Association for Social Engineering, Research, and Training (ASSERT), a registered society dedicated to developing human resources and transforming society socio-economically through research, training, counseling, and consulting.

Jerome Winston is at the Royal Melbourne Institute of Technology, Australia, where he developed and continues to lead the graduate diploma program in human services research monitoring and evaluation. He helped found the Australasian Evaluation Society and currently serves on the Committee on Ethics and Standards in Evaluation.

Please note two points. First, we have grouped together the commentaries of Duncan, Ginsberg, and Rugh. As recent or current chairs of the AEA's Topical Interest Group on International and Cross-Cultural Evaluation, these three evaluators developed a document entitled "Guidelines for International and Cross-Cultural Evaluations," which included comments on the Guiding Principles. In addition, they provided their collective reactions to particular subparts of several principles, and those reactions are included below.

Second, Sharp developed his commentary for this chapter partly by soliciting input from the other members of the Australasian Evaluation Society's Committee on Ethics and Standards in Evaluation. Committee members whose views Sharp incorporated into his commentary include Kerry Rose (senior review officer, Department of Education, Queensland), Anthea Rutter (planning and research officer, Western Metropolitan College of TAFE, Victoria), Ralph Straton (director, Institute for Social Programme Evaluation, Murdoch University, Murdoch), Ian Trotman (Chief Executive's Branch, State Services Commission, Wellington, New Zealand), and Jerome Winston, who also provided a separate commentary.

Overall Applicability

BEMELMANS-VIDEC: I have read the principles with great interest and find them to be both clear and exhaustive. They touch the core of the dilemmas that evaluators should face and give sound substantial and procedural guidance.

SINGH: I found it pithy, concise and clear. The guidelines for evaluators in general would also be applicable to evaluators in the developing societies.

LOVE: I applaud the work of the AEA task force in drafting the principles. I feel strongly that the professional evaluation associations must take a leadership role regarding evaluation standards and ethical guidelines.

COOLEY: In general, I found the guidelines to be both applicable and—perhaps an even sterner test—useful. Clearly, a great deal of thought has gone into their articulation.

HJELHOLT: The AEA task force has done good work and apparently discussed a lot of questions and difficulties in the evaluation process. They come up with the five principles, which in my summary are: (1) Try to do as competent, professional work as possible in the given situation; (2) Try to act honest and decent towards those you encounter in the process; (3) Try not to get caught up in the power struggles in society; let your conscience guide you.

SINHA: The guidelines are very comprehensive and are precisely written. I can hardly add or subtract anything. However, I do wonder how Indian evaluators can follow the guidelines. Things are pretty stabilized in your world. All stakeholders—evaluators, those who ask for evaluation, and the general public—share certain norms. They pertain to objectivity, impersonalized relationships, and surveillance. Evaluation in India, and maybe in other developing countries, is a recent phenomenon. Aims and objectives of many projects are so broadly or vaguely defined, or the gestation period is so long, that it becomes difficult to agree on the criteria for evaluation. At times projects are launched for objectives which are qualitatively different from the ones which are professed in the document.

SHARP: There are some in Australasia who take issue with the use of the term "Evaluator" in the Australian context and who are concerned about the restrictive or elitist connotation of "professionalisation" of evaluation. The AEA's Guiding Principles share the clear assumption . . . that "evaluation is a profession" and the "principles are broadly intended to cover all kinds of evaluation." However, the term Evaluator soon dominates the focus, with a tacit assumption of a narrow role of external independent evaluation consultant in mind. This may be a result of (what is perceived from afar as) the growth of an industry of externally funded evaluations in the USA.

LOVE: Although the principles are generally relevant to my work, for me the important question is whether or not the principles will serve as a useful guide for practice. To do so, the principles must help resolve practice dilemmas caused by conflicting principles. I think the next step is to guide practitioners by presenting the relative importance of each principle together with a decision-making model. This will be a more useful guide for practice and a more effective tool for teaching evaluation.

HJELHOLT: Too many evaluators forget that our "technique" comes out of the North-Western science-culture, and we then act as if this culture is in the society we operate in.

WINSTON: I have noticed that what is a guiding principle in one country/region is often not even considered relevant in another. This may be because conditions differ; it may also be because of the extent to which evaluation practitioners and program managers become isolated from people doing much the same kind of work in the next state or country. It may also be the result of the way evaluation has developed in the different countries. In some countries, it is a profession led primarily by academics; in other countries, it is a profession led by people who are employed in departments and agencies that do and use evaluation.

RWAMPORORO: I fully agree with all the five principles laid out, as far as their applicability in the North American context is concerned. However, adjustment to some statements will have to be made in order to make a provision for existing conditions in the African setting. . . . Therefore, from the perspective of international evaluation, other general issues which make the developing country scenario different from the North American situation include: the state of infrastructural development (that is, the road network, telecommunication facilities) and the degree of development of democracies. These will inevitably affect the practice of evaluators. Needless to say, the guiding principles will be a good benchmark to fall back upon in either case.

HJELHOLT: The importance of guiding principles for a profession lies in the process of formulating them as it makes the profession conscious of the values which guide it. Therefore [I agree with] the importance of the task force's recommendation of continued work to support development of principles.

LOVE: The principles reflect the U.S. cultural context or perhaps more accurately, the U.S. evaluation sub-cultural context! Even within the U.S., the principles do not reflect well enough the realities of internal evaluators, who may be both part-time evaluators and who have unique demands placed on them by the organizational working environment, or evaluators in "grass roots" subcultures, such as those experienced in many non-profit organizations.

SHARP: There is much to gain in developing a relevant approach to ethics and standards for the purchasers and users of evaluation, as well as the Professional Evaluator. There may be more to lose by not recognizing the significant differences in evaluation in different contexts, across countries and cultures. The opportunity for collaboration and to comment on these policies among the various evaluation groups is a step in the right direction.

Comments on Specific Principles

III.A. *Systematic Inquiry*

RWAMPORORO: I have highlighted data-based because this would only hold true in the North American context, while lack of data in most developing country settings would constrain this important principle. I am therefore of the view that a provision should be made for the use of "case studies or anecdotal information" where data sources have not yet been fully developed. From my experience in this area, this approach may help enrich an evaluation even for data-deficient programs. Unfortunately, most evaluations are currently being done on programs that were not results-oriented initially, and therefore had not stressed data collection activities as part of the program outputs.

SINHA: There is a recent trend in India: the evaluation report has to be reader-friendly, which actually means descriptive, observational, and non-technical. In reality it discriminates against those social scientists who have the competence to use rigorous methods and favors those who can give positive strokes. Thus a cleavage is developing between the technically sound social scientists and the operators who write acceptable evaluation. The latter, of course, are sought after more than the former. They even downgrade the former as too technical, fussy, and unreceptive to the needs of the clients.

III.B. Competence

SINGH: There are hardly any formal avenues for improvement in competencies. Though the principles are applicable to the developing societies, their ranking may vary. I would rank [their order of importance] as follows: (1) competence, (2) systematic inquiry, (3) respect for people, (4) integrity/honesty, and (5) responsibilities for general and public welfare. The reasons for the new ranking are that we do not have skilled and trained evaluators, which is a major bottleneck for the profession.

SINHA: Because of a variety of developmental activities, a number of government, international, and private funding agencies need evaluators. The opportunities have raised many evaluators who are more interested in the resources than the outcomes of evaluation. They have indifferent competence. In a culture where personalized relationships and connections matter more than public interests, a nexus develops where evaluation is a means to bestow favors to each other irrespective of their levels of competence.

LOVE: In my opinion, the major obstacles encountered in developing standards/ethics for evaluation is the diverse disciplinary backgrounds and training of evaluators and the equally diverse locations of practice. As a result, I think that the principles represent a realistic developmental phase that temporarily bypasses these obstacles. I see the AEA principles as being "umbrella" principles (that is, generally applicable and general consensus) that can be used as a guide to the development of more specific standards for particular areas of evaluation practice (for example, educational evaluation). The principles have the potential, therefore, of promoting consistency and conceptual cohesiveness in future standards documents, while at the same time strengthening the identity of evaluators and the quality of evaluation practice.

DUNCAN/GINSBERG/RUGH: Include cultural competence as one aspect of evaluation which evaluators "should continually seek to maintain and improve."

III.C. Integrity/Honesty

RWAMPORORO: I have personal reservations [about this principle], but you do not have to take them seriously. If these principles are to be applied across the board, I would question whether professional ethics for developing country counterparts, which are still on a shaky foundation, would adhere to this principle.

BEMELMANS-VIDEC: The uses of data resulting from a specific evaluation are discussed. Would it not be wise to advise evaluators to make firm arrangements with their clients about this vital issue when making up the research contract?

SINHA: Evaluators are quite often totally dependent for their survival on the funding agencies which call for evaluation. Quite often funding agencies are themselves accountable to those who raise money for them, although they are not quite knowledgeable about the local conditions. In such cases, the survival of not only the evaluators, but the funding agencies and their projects depend on a positive evaluation. As a result, those who call for an evaluation take the care to identify an evaluator who can appreciate the contingencies involved.

BEMELMANS-VIDEC: I would suggest that a significant conflict of interest should induce the evaluator not to accept the invitation to do an evaluation.

COOLEY: While ostensibly reasonable and defensible, [this principle] is not consistent with standard practice in our industry. Such potential conflicts are, as a matter of principle and practice, discussed with clients in selecting evaluators but are not reiterated in evaluation reports.

BEMELMANS-VIDEC: [Regarding] prevention of substantial misuse of the evaluator's work: this should also be guaranteed in the initial negotiating phase when the object of the evaluation, the users/stakeholders, and the function of the report (who is to decide on the use of the results), and so on should be explicitly mentioned.

III.D. Respect for People

SINGH: [My choice for third-most important principle] goes to respect for people, for the developing societies are diverse and heterogeneous in nature. Evaluators, therefore, should be sensitive to social, cultural, and economic differences among different stakeholders. They will not only have to understand how their background would affect their interaction with different stakeholders, but also to consider its impact on their findings.

DUNCAN/GINSBERG/RUGH: Differences (culture, religion, gender, and so on) which "matter" will be different in different cultures.

III.E. Responsibilities for General and Public Welfare

DUNCAN/GINSBERG/RUGH: If resources are not adequate, is it ethical to undertake the evaluation?

SINGH: I have observed that researchers and evaluators are not responsive to needs and rights of respondents of their studies. The respondents never get any feedback from the researchers, which may lead to negative feelings among the respondents about the research process itself. It would be nice if guiding principles focus in greater detail on certain needs and rights of respondents (it also includes other sources of information) and evaluators' obligations to them.

LOVE: In Canada, where a greater proportion of our evaluators may work for government, the cultural context of the Westminster system of government influences the application and relative weighing of the principles. Likewise, in some Commonwealth situations, the Minister (politician) is clearly the primary evaluation client and this fact, coupled with a Code of Conduct for civil servants, alters the way some of the principles can be applied. In non-Western (or non-Northern) evaluation contexts, concern for equity and controlling access to the power of evaluative information also may strongly influence the way the principles are applied.

SHARP: While it is no doubt a laudable human right to freedom, there are significant differences in the ways countries and cultures articulate their discretions and responsibilities which are not represented in the way the American Constitution conceives of rights or freedom. These assumptions of American values and rights are implicit or explicit in the AEA's document, and make its translation to other countries and cultures of limited relevance. Australia is a democratic country with a Freedom of Information Act. However, it would be difficult (even under this Act) to "allow all relevant stakeholders to have access to evaluative information, and . . . actively disseminate that information to stakeholders." Unlike the American Constitution, Australia's Constitution does not include a "Bill of Rights" but relies mainly on English "Common Law" and specific acts and regulations to deal with social justice issues. However, Australia does have strict rules about the rights of human subjects to informed consent about the processes which will involve them. Informed consent of participants in research is now a mandatory requirement of research designs in University- and Government-funded programs. This raises issues regarding the management of evaluation projects which most Managers and Evaluation Advisors would not have the training nor patience, under usual circumstances, to solve.

COOLEY: This principle poses some potential difficulties in practice. It is the accepted norm in our industry that the organization that sponsors an evaluation "owns" it and controls its distribution. Although we have occasionally felt that this practice limited free disclosure of information, I see no obvious resolution and feel that, in the absence of such a resolution, the implications of accepting such a guideline as a professional or ethical obligation needs to be carefully considered.

HJELHOLT: In September we had an election to parliament here in Denmark. It was decided by the man responsible for an ongoing evaluation of economic development to postpone the results of the study until the election was over. He felt that the results would be misused by the press, politicians, opposition, and government in the election campaigns and that findings would be taken out of their context. When it was found out that the results had been in before election day, he was severely clobbered for having made a "political decision." In my mind he had tried to follow this principle. But the case shows that two of the important factors for evaluators—the media and the politicians—are not easy to handle anywhere. You have not much protection or say in the use of the findings. Your reservations, limitation of the studies, and so on are lost in either the political discussions or in the media coverage.

BEMELMANS-VIDEC: Here the evaluator is depicted as someone involved with a public function, with a function that touches general social interests. . . . I find this a very important point; the fact that we touch at social interests is a primary condition for professionalization. The evaluator faces the same dilemmas as the public servant who has to mediate between various interests in an attempt to act "in the general interest." What should be the key in that mediating process? In other words, what should be the final values and norms that guide the evaluator in this process?. . . In so doing, where lies the evaluator's final loyalty? With the client? An illustrative point: What should an evaluator do when (s)he encounters fraud or other forms of irregular/illegal behaviour while doing an evaluation?

COOLEY: [This topic] is frequently discussed in the international evaluation arena. In addition to the implication noted in the document, this guideline has consequences with respect to potential divergences between the perspectives, interests, and needs of sponsors of evaluation, on the one hand, and the broader public interest, on the other. In our experience, such issues are best negotiated and addressed as part of the initial understanding between evaluator and sponsor. It may be unrealistic, however, that evaluators' judgment regarding the public interest can or should entirely supersede sponsors' perspectives on these same issues should a difference of opinion emerge subsequent to such initial agreements.

Comments Cutting Across Principles

COOLEY: The concept of the "client" is somewhat complicated in the case of such evaluations, inasmuch as a donor organization is frequently funding the evaluation but may share implementation and funding responsibility with several other entities, including the host country. In certain of these cases, it is important to draw an operational distinction between "client" and "sponsor." Where this is the case, some of the statements in the guidelines regarding clients would appear to be better directed to sponsors.

HJELHOLT: The difficulties arise especially when we come to evaluation of development projects in "the third or fourth world." And here we get caught in the dilemma about "clients." Who is the client? The Western development agency which usually funds the evaluation, pays our salaries? Or the third-world country, the poor peasants? Here you as an evaluator really can get squeezed. You remember the fate of the Indian national Monitoring and Evaluation Group (MEG)? I was a member of it for five years till it was abolished after pressures from Western countries. They threatened the Indian government by withholding money for development (foreign currency) if the group did not stop its evaluation of the role which the foreign development agencies played in the process. When the clients are two different cultures and the main actors are politicians and bureaucrats, you are up against forces which put strain on all your principles and you only have your own conscience to guide you.

SINHA: Had we got an association like AEA, it could have enforced some norms. But . . . people biochemically reject and undermine such efforts. An association is not in their interest. In sum, all three main stakeholders advertently or inadvertently collude to create a situation where the AEA guidelines look ideal but distant to our realities.

SINGH: There is hardly any professional association of evaluators in the developing countries. Evaluators work as individual professionals. Further, they are more concerned about growth of evaluation activity at this point of time rather than evaluation as a profession. Even if they are, they would look towards AEA for ethical guidelines. Here, it would not be irrelevant to mention that as the number of evaluators is less, there is no critical mass to advance the profession. . . . In Delhi, we do not have more than twenty to twenty-five evaluators.

Important Topics Not Addressed

COOLEY: An important, though frequently under-emphasized element in the evaluation of international development programs is building the capacity of host country governments and institutions to evaluate their own performance. The guidelines are silent on the issue of capacity building, which I would imagine could be an important issue domestically as well.

SHARP: While agreeing with the educational and leadership function of such Guiding Principles, it is also possible to conceive of other implications of the focus on big-"E" Evaluators in the AEA's document. If the AEA meant to follow other "Professions" or guilds and to delineate a specific professional elite (that is, the big-"E" Evaluators), then surely it would need to address the issue of sanctions and membership restrictions to sustain quality assurance of the membership. This is touched on in the section on Competence of Evaluators. . . . These approaches would not be welcomed, nor would they be practical, in Australia. Also there is a danger, in the AEA's approach, of appearing to focus only on the needs and behaviour of the evaluation practitioner, which could be seen to be irrelevant or unconvincing to the commissioners (purchasers) of evaluation, such as government agencies.

COOLEY: Implicit in the guidelines is the notion of independent evaluators, working directly for a client. In the context of international development evaluation, such individuals are normally contracted through firms who are responsible for issuance of final reports. In our case, we typically regard the final evaluation as a corporate product and de-emphasize somewhat the sense of the evaluators as free agents who simply happen to be contracted through the firm. While we would be very reluctant to amplify the findings or modify the conclusions reached by an evaluation team, we do see the firm as having the ultimate responsibility for ensuring that the guidelines are met and that the evaluation meets client and contractual needs.

LOVE: The principles are an excellent starting point for dialogue. I think the task force should go the next step by articulating the relative weights of each principle and a decision-making model after consulting a broad cross-section of evaluators. This could be repeated by the major evaluation associations to get a better reading of how universally applicable the principles may be. This could lead to the creation of guidelines or standards for specific fields of practices (for example, government) by evaluators in those areas of service and for different cultural settings.

COOLEY: Although the concept of outside evaluators implicit in the guidelines is the norm in international as well as domestic evaluation, there is growing acceptance of "fourth generation evaluation" whereby the evaluative exercise is done in a collaborative fashion and is seen as part of an ongoing management improvement process. The guidelines would appear to be relatively silent on this type of evaluation and the implications for ethical standards of evaluators.

Conclusion

In the previous section, we presented the comments from our twelve international evaluators in such a way as to allow their individual voices to speak out about individual principles. In this final section we ask what those voices say when we listen to them in unison. In other words, what are the consolidated messages from our international commentators?

Overall, it seems that the commentators generally find the principles to be useful. Although some commentators have some misgivings, they generally see the principles as a useful discussion document, raising important issues. All found the document to be generally clear and thought provoking.

The commentators—whether from developing or developed countries—also seem to agree, however, that the principles are definitely tied to U.S. cultural realities and to a general belief in the operation of democratic processes. In different cultural and political contexts, the relevance and applicability of the principles become more tenuous. It is clear, for instance, that evaluation is a new area for most developing countries; consequently, the degree of professionalization which exists in the United States and other developed countries does not exist in most developing countries.

Issues such as competence levels, professional associations, evaluation contracts/documents, and others are simply not salient topics among evaluators in developing countries. This does not mean that these issues are unimportant or that principles about them are not a good idea. Rather, there are simply different, more pressing issues for evaluators in developing countries, in particular the day-to-day realities of implementing evaluation of any type in contexts where the infrastructure, both physical and professional, is absent or underdeveloped.

Nonetheless, the commentators highlight a number of important issues that evaluators based in the United States could consider in more detail. First, the principles seem more tied to certain types of evaluators (for example, external independent evaluators) than to other types (internal evaluators or manager-evaluators). Second, the definition of "client" is a difficult issue, one that cannot be easily generalized across evaluation projects or settings or even across time within the same project. Third, the uses and misuses of evaluators' work is a critical issue that the principles begin to touch upon but not in enough detail. Fourth, the principles do not go far enough in discussing the conditions under which evaluators should refuse an assignment. Finally, the commentators also raise some issues about which the principles are silent, including evaluation capacity building and procedures for reconciling conflicts between and among principles.

The AEA task force that drafted the Guiding Principles recognized that its job was not done with the distribution of the final document. Indeed, they noted as one of their assumptions that "These principles are part of an evolving process of self-examination by the profession and should be revisited on a regular basis." We believe that the commentaries of these twelve international evaluators raise important issues for further reflection as this "self-examination" process continues within the AEA or begins in other professional associations (for example, Australasian Evaluation Society, Canadian Evaluation Society, European Evaluation Society).

Furthermore, the utility of the comments by evaluators from developing countries suggests that developed-country professional associations would benefit greatly from a regular channel of communication and feedback with developing-country evaluators. Developing-country evaluators would also benefit from these ongoing dialogues as a way to learn how other evaluators have addressed issues they themselves may be facing now or in the near future.

References

American Evaluation Association. *Guiding Principles for Evaluators*. Charlottesville, Va.: American Evaluation Association, 1994.

Conner, R. F., and Hendricks, M. (eds.). *International Innovations in Evaluation Methodology*. New Directions for Program Evaluation, no. 42. San Francisco: Jossey-Bass, 1989.

Cook, T. D., and Campbell, D. T. *Quasi-Experimentation: Design and Analysis Issues for Field Settings*. Chicago: Rand McNally, 1979.

Patton, M. W. *Qualitative Evaluation and Research Methods*. Newbury Park, Calif.: Sage, 1990.

Posavac, E. J., and Carey, R. G. *Program Evaluation: Methods and Case Studies*. Englewood Cliffs, N.J.: Prentice-Hall, 1989.

Rossi, P. H., and Freeman, H. E. *Evaluation: A Systematic Approach*. (5th ed.) Newbury Park, Calif.: Sage, 1993.

MICHAEL HENDRICKS is an independent consultant in Washington, D.C., specializing in program planning and evaluation, organizational development, and technical assistance and training.

ROSS F. CONNER is associate professor of urban and regional planning, School of Social Ecology, and associate professor of medicine, Department of Medicine, School of Medicine at the University of California, Irvine.

Drawing on literature from the field of ethics in research and on multicultural, feminist ethical principles, the author explores methodological implications for evaluation practice.

Identifying and Respecting Differences Among Participants in Evaluation Studies

Donna M. Mertens

The themes of empowerment and social justice have surfaced in the evaluation community along with a recognition that large groups of people do not have power and, as a consequence, experience oppression. The American Evaluation Association's principle III.D.5, in the category of "Respect for People," focuses on this issue. It reads:

> Evaluators have the responsibility to identify and respect differences among participants, such as differences in their culture, religion, gender, disability, age, sexual orientation, and ethnicity, and to be mindful of potential implications of these differences when planning, conducting, analyzing, and reporting their evaluations.

In this chapter I explore the meaning of this principle for evaluators as a response to the task force's invitation to participate in the evolving process of self-examination of the principles by the profession, especially in light of the acknowledged limitation that these principles were developed in the context of Western culture and may have different relevance in other cultures and across subcultures within the United States. I chose this principle as my point of departure because of its relevance to the themes of empowerment and social justice in evaluation work and to emphasize that actualizing this principle has pervasive implications for AEA's Guiding Principles. This principle concerning diversity and inclusion has implications not only at the level of identifying and respecting the viewpoints of marginalized groups, but also for the technical adequacy of what evaluators do. For example, Stanfield (1993) stated that ideological intrusions and cultural biases make data validity and reliability problematic and controversial. Evaluators need to reflect on how to address validity and reliability honestly in a cultural context, so as not to violate human rights of the culturally oppressed.

Emancipatory Framework

I use the views on ethics of feminists, ethnic minorities, poor people, and persons with disabilities to explore the meaning of identifying and respecting differences among participants in evaluation studies (Madison, 1992; Mertens and McLaughlin, 1995). I draw upon literature from the field of ethics in research, as there is not yet an extensive body of writing by feminists, minorities, and persons with disabilities on ethics in evaluation. I recognize that evaluators often work under constraints different from those of researchers. Therefore, as part of my discussion of multicultural, feminist ethical principles, I pose questions about their application to evaluation. I recognize that many different viewpoints are espoused by these diverse groups. However, they do share some underlying orientations, and it is on this core of relative commonalities that I focus.

Scholars writing from the perspectives of feminists, ethnic minorities, poor people, and people with disabilities have commonly expressed dissatisfaction with both the positivist and interpretivist paradigms of inquiry, arguing that an emancipatory framework is more appropriate to stop oppression and bring about social justice (Lather, 1992; Mertens, Farley, Madison, and Singleton, 1994; Oliver, 1992; Steady, 1993). Three characteristics separate the emancipatory framework from those more traditionally used in evaluation: (1) recognition of silenced voices, ensuring that groups traditionally marginalized in society are equally "heard" during the evaluation process and formation of evaluation findings and recommendations; (2) analysis of power inequities in terms of the social relationships involved in the planning, implementation, and reporting of evaluations; (3) linking evaluation results to political action. In the next sections, I explore these three distinguishing features in more depth in the context of multicultural, feminist principles of ethics in evaluation.

Recognition of Silenced Voices

Reinharz stated: "Diversity has become a new criterion for feminist research excellence" (1992, p. 253). By this, she means inclusion to the maximum extent possible, as representative as the available resources will permit, variations as to age, economic class, race, religion, ethnicity, gender, and differential abilities. Thus, this directs evaluators to reject a narrow, biased viewpoint, such as that represented by white, middle-class, abled values, and to include the perspectives of everyone, no matter what their race, class, sexual preference, gender, and abilities.

Harding (1993) addressed the topic of inclusion of persons with marginalized lives in her proposal of three standards for excellence in research. Does it start with marginalized lives? Do you talk to persons in marginalized groups? Do you meaningfully involve affected people in the planning of research?

Zarb (1992) proposed a set of questions that parallels and extends Harding's, in reference to his work with persons with disabilities. What opportunities exist for self-reflection and mutual sharing of experience between researchers and people with disabilities? How far have we come in involving people with disabilities in the research process? What opportunities exist for people with disabilities to criticize the research and influence future directions? What happens to the products of the research?

Evaluators are cautioned to recognize the diversity that exists within groups, and that individuals hold multiple stances simultaneously, such as race, gender, class, disability, and sexual orientation (Brewer, 1993; Pollard, 1992). Pollard (1992) warned against assuming that all people who share a particular characteristic (such as gender) share the same concerns. Making this assumption results in excluding those with different concerns. For example, the feminist movement has been criticized for focusing on the concerns of white, middle-class women. If the focus is only on gender, then race becomes invisible. Pollard supported the notion of cultural variance, that is, a celebration of pluralism. She recommended that researchers include in their studies women and girls who represent various cultures, classes, physical abilities, and sexual orientations in a way that reflects the voices of members of these groups, and that researchers examine the ways women connect and move between the multiple statuses that they hold.

Analysis of Power Inequities

The assumption made in participatory models of evaluation is that inclusion of relevant stakeholder groups will ensure that evaluation findings and the utilization of those findings will respond to those groups whose influence has traditionally been marginalized in today's society (Mertens, Farley, Madison, and Singleton, 1994). The emancipatory framework recognizes that mere participation is not sufficient, and that it is necessary to analyze the power inequities that function to silence their voices, even after their opinions have been solicited and expressed.

Zarb (1992) continued his line of questioning within an emancipatory framework to analyze power inequities in social relations surrounding disability research. Who controls what the research will be about and how it will be carried out? How alienating are existing research practices, and how can alienated research be transformed? What does or could research contribute to the empowerment of people with disabilities?

Pollard (1992) emphasized the need to teach those who are oppressed (in particular, women of color) how to access the sources of power and privilege in society. Terry (1993) used the image of America as being controlled by a "white male club" to explore the cultural and institutional dynamics in this country that distribute influence and power among its members (white, male, middle class, and able bodied), and the members' use of that power to dominate groups unlike itself (that is, women, minorities, poor people, and people with disabilities). He suggested several questions as a guide to analyzing power inequities in a research study. Who has access to societal resources? Are the resources equitably distributed? Who holds power, and who can marshall the resources to accomplish a goal? What are the institutionalized patterns and practices of the (white male) club? What are the dominant and persistent cultural values and assumptions of the club? Evaluators could use these questions to analyze power relationships in the programs that they study by recognizing that those who belong to the club (that is, those who are in power) have access to the resources. Evaluators should be aware of institutionalized patterns and practices that serve to buttress power inequities, such as seniority systems, selection of textbooks, hiring and promotion practice, and educational testing and tracking. In addition, specific cultural values and assumptions should be made explicit, such as using ethnocentric standards to define what is acceptable, denigrating alternative value orientations (such as collaboration versus competition), and misplacing the problem by blaming the victim.

Evaluators (and the people who pay them to do their work) hold considerable power in the design and conduct of evaluation studies in terms of identification of the theoretical framework that guides a program, development of appropriate evaluation questions, decisions about and implementation of data collection methods, and the analysis, interpretation, and use of the results. An examination of ethics within an emancipatory framework provides direction for methodology that can be more responsive to diversity and less oppressive.

Program Theory and Evaluation Questions. Villegas (1991) discussed how the development of research questions is derived from the program theory that is operating in the minds of the researchers and the influence of cultural bias on this conceptualization. For example, Villegas illustrated how various explanations of differential achievement by minority students emanated from different theoretical perspectives on the nature of the problem. If the researcher/evaluator used a cultural deficit theory that placed the problem "in the child" or "in the family," then the corresponding evaluation questions might be: Is there a higher rate of single-parent families among minorities? How do black and white parents compare in discipline techniques? However, if the evaluator used an emancipatory framework that saw power inequities at the root of the problem, then the evaluation question might be: How can we teach minority students so they do not continue to be oppressed?

Data Collection Decisions. Oliver (1992) noted the influence of theoretical frameworks on data collection decisions by providing contrasting examples of survey questions used by researchers who believed that the problem is "in the person" with disabilities versus one who believed that the problem is one of power inequities. He cited two questions asked by the British government in their survey of persons with disabilities (Martin, Melzer, and Elliott,

1988; Martin and White, 1988) as exemplifying the positivist perspective that the problem is in the person: Are your difficulties in understanding people mainly due to a hearing problem? Have you attended a special school because of a long-term health problem or disability? In contrast, he cited questions that could have been asked if the study had used an emancipatory framework: Are your difficulties in understanding people mainly due to their inabilities to communicate with you? Have you attended a special school because of your education authority's policy of sending people with your health problem or disability to such places? Use of questions that locate the problem in the person results in a feeling of alienation on the part of the person being interviewed and in findings that are not relevant or useful to the persons experiencing oppression. Foster (1993a) and Barnes (1992) also discussed strategies related to interviewing persons with disabilities that emphasize the participant's control in the interview session to open or close topics, raise issues that are critical, and to extend the conversation or bring it to an early conclusion.

Reporting Evaluation Findings. Cook and Fonow (1990) discussed ethical issues that arise from the use of language as a means to subordinate women, such as by the use of masculine pronouns, application of offensive adjectives to women's experiences, and the subsumption of women under male categories. Parallels exist in the writings of minorities about race research, for example, defining single mothers as a moral/social problem (broken home) when it applies to minority women but as alternative family structures when it applies to white women. Stanfield (1993) noted that how elites talk and write has a profound role in reproducing the racial order of things. Social science discourse involves an elite way of talking and writing that in race-centered societies creates a public image of the "dominant" and the "oppressed" that appear to be objective and value free. Oppressive use of language persists in the identification of persons with disabilities. Even the word disability is negative, defined in terms of what a person *can't* do. In the area of deafness, deaf people prefer to be thought of as a cultural group that uses visual-gestural communication, not as a group who *can't* hear (Singleton, 1993).

Link to Political Action

Evaluators have long been cognizant of the importance of utilization of their findings. Therefore, there is much similarity in the stance that evaluators have espoused in terms of ensuring utilization and the emancipatory framework link between research results and political action. The key difference, which needs to be emphasized, is that the persons who are most marginalized, oppressed, or with the least power, traditionally, should be at the center of plans for action. They should be included in discussions of how they can change their own lives by the use of the results from the study. The precise role of the evaluator in such a context is yet to be defined.

A mutual interactive learning process is required for effective political action. First, the evaluator must be sensitized to the recommendations for action that the oppressed groups believe are appropriate for them. Second, the members of the oppressed groups must learn ways to use the information to change their own lives. Third, policy makers must be accepting of intervention strategies that emanate from the perspectives of those for whom the social policy intervention is designed.

Questions Remain

Feminists, minorities, poor people, and persons with disabilities have expressed their belief that an emancipatory approach to social inquiry will lead to the elimination of discrimination and oppression, and to a transformation of all spheres of society (Steady, 1993). Emancipatory evaluation is about the systematic demystification of the structures and processes that create oppression and the establishment of a workable dialogue between the evaluation community and oppressed people in order to facilitate the latter's empowerment. To do this, evaluators must learn how to put their knowledge and skills at the disposal of oppressed people (Barnes, 1992; Oliver, 1992). Yet evaluators work in the real world, with real constraints that present challenges to the implementation of an emancipatory approach in their work. Many questions remain concerning the roles and responsibilities of evaluators. To begin with, evaluators must ask themselves: Do I *want* to do emancipatory evaluations? Do I want to relinquish control of my work to others? (Foster, 1993b).

Other important questions remain. What are the consequences of doing evaluation within an emancipatory paradigm? What are the consequences of *not* doing evaluation within this paradigm? What are the changes that would occur in the roles of evaluators in an emancipatory study? Would emancipatory evaluators adopt the role of facilitators, thus removing themselves from control over the design, implementation, interpretation, and dissemination of their work? What effects might occur with regard to the technical quality of the data collected in an emancipatory evaluation? What are the potential problems in the actual process of collecting data? Is undertaking evaluation with an explicitly political agenda undermining the evaluation process? (Foster, 1993b; Mertens, Farley, Madison, and Singleton, 1994).

Clearly, a longer list of questions could be generated. My hope is that the evaluation community will hear the voices of those who have been traditionally silenced and will seek ways to become part of the solution to the problems of oppression and social injustice.

References

Barnes, C. "Qualitative Research: Valuable or Irrelevant?" *Disability, Handicap, and Society*, 1992, 7 (2), 115–124.

Brewer, R. M. "Theorizing Race, Class, and Gender." In S. M. James and A.P.A. Busia (eds.), *Theorizing Black Feminisms*. London: Routledge, 1993.

Cook, J. A., and Fonow, M. M. "Knowledge and Women's Interests: Issues of Epistemology and Methodology in Feminist Sociological Research." In J. M. Nielsen (ed.), *Feminist Research Methods: Exemplary Readings in the Social Sciences*. Boulder, Colo.: Westview Press, 1990.

Foster, S. "Outsider in the Deaf World: Reflections of an Ethnographic Researcher." Paper presented at the annual meeting of the American Educational Research Association, Atlanta, Apr., 1993a.

Foster, S. "Ethnographic Interviews in Disability Studies: The Case of Research with People Who Are Deaf." Paper presented at the conference of the American Sociological Association, Miami, Fla., Aug., 1993b.

Harding, S. "Gender, Method, and Knowledge: New Issues." Paper presented at the annual meeting of the American Educational Research Association, Atlanta, Apr., 1993.

Lather, P. "Critical Frames in Educational Research: Feminist and Poststructural Perspectives." *Theory Into Practice*, 1992, *31* (2), 1–13.

Madison, A. M. (ed.). *Minority Issues in Program Evaluation*. San Francisco: Jossey-Bass, 1992.

Martin, J., and White, A. *The Financial Circumstances of Disabled Adults in Private Households*. London: HMSO, 1988.

Mertens, D. M., and McLaughlin, J. *Research Methods in Special Education*. Newbury Park, Calif.: Sage, 1995.

Mertens, D. M., Farley, J., Madison, A. M., and Singleton, P. "Diverse Voices in Evaluation Practice: Feminists, Minorities, and Persons with Disabilities." *Evaluation Practice*, 1994, *15* (2), 123–129.

Oliver, M. "Changing the Social Relations of Research Production?" *Disability, Handicap, and Society*, 1992, *7* (2), 101–114.

Pollard, D. S. "Toward a Pluralistic Perspective on Equity." *Women's Education Equity Act Publishing Center Digest*, February 1992, p. 1–2, 7.

Reinharz, S. *Feminist Methods in Social Research*. New York: Oxford University Press, 1992.

Singleton, P. "Evaluation Perspectives of a Deaf Feminist." Paper presented at the annual meeting of the American Evaluation Association, Dallas, Tex., Nov., 1993.

Stanfield, J. H. "Methodological Reflections." In J. H. Stanfield and R. M. Dennis (eds.), *Race and Ethnicity in Research Methods*. Newbury Park, Calif.: Sage, 1993.

Steady, F. C. "Women and Collective Action." In S. M. James and A.P.A. Busia (eds.), *Theorizing Black Feminisms*. London: Routledge, 1993.

Terry, R. "The White Male Club: Biology and Power." In J. Andrzejewski (ed.), *Oppression and Social Justice: Critical Frameworks*. (4th ed.) Needham Heights, Mass.: Gerin Press, 1993.

Villegas, A. M. *Culturally Responsive Pedagogy for the 1990s and Beyond*. Princeton, N.J.: Educational Testing Service, 1991.

Zarb, G. "On the Road to Damascus: First Steps Towards Changing the Relations of Disability Research Production." *Disability, Handicap, and Society*, 1992, *7* (2), 125–138.

DONNA M. MERTENS is professor in educational foundations and research, Gallaudet University, Washington, D.C.

The author presents an agenda of issues related to the future development of ethics in evaluation and suggests initial steps in addressing these issues, emphasizing the role of evaluators, clients, and organizations supporting evaluation.

The Future of Ethics in Evaluation: Developing the Dialogue

Dianna L. Newman

The work of developing ethical practices in evaluation has just begun. The Guiding Principles are designed to be living statements that will grow and change with the role of evaluators and evaluation. This chapter presents a tentative agenda of issues related to the development and practice of ethical evaluation, followed by some suggestions as to how the American Evaluation Association, evaluators, trainers of evaluators, and clients can be involved in this development.

Agenda of Ethical Issues in Evaluation

An examination of current topics pertaining to the development of evaluation reveals several issues that will affect the development of an ethic of evaluation. What constitutes ethical practice is already under consideration in some of these issues; for others the dialogue is only beginning. In many cases, the developers of the principles agreed to disagree on the ethical impact of an issue, in hopes that the living nature of the document and the continuing development of the profession would more clearly focus and define the problem and its resolution.

Alternate Roles of Evaluators. Literature on the functions of evaluators indicates that they are perceived as fulfilling multiple roles with many diverse and frequently conflicting expectations. Among the more common roles identified are those related to tasks associated with the process of evaluation: data collector/researcher, manager or administrator, and reporter. Each role carries with it expectations of appropriate practice as perceived by the evaluator, the client, and stakeholders. Typical expectations of the evaluator as data collector/

researcher include objectivity, adequate knowledge of measurement and analysis techniques, fair and reliable collection of information, balanced collection of viewpoints, and the ability to cooperate with program staff. Expectations of evaluators as administrators reflect project management, fiscal responsibility, ability to communicate with the client, and focusing of evaluation to reflect client needs. Report writers are expected to provide balanced information, clear and concise summaries that reflect client concerns, and timely results.

On the basis of these expectations, ethical conflicts occur in multiple ways. First, the evaluator, client, and other stakeholders may have differing definitions of what these expectations mean within each role. For example, an evaluator may perceive that a random sample of parent opinions will provide balanced, representative information on the success of a new cooperative learning curriculum; parents opposed to the program, however, may want special input from their interest group. Second, even though they may agree on expected functions, evaluators, clients, and stakeholders may differ according to the priority of expectations within a role. Evaluators may perceive that a balanced report is most important, whereas decision makers may perceive timeliness of information to be of greatest value. Third, ethical dilemmas may occur among the roles of the evaluator for the evaluator. The evaluator in an administrative managerial role may be concerned with the fiscal aspects of the evaluation, such as cost of surveys, staff time, and commitment to other projects; the evaluator as researcher/data collector may place priority on the representativeness of the data and adequate development of instruments; at the same time, expectations of the reporter role urge timeliness of information in favor of cost factors.

Other roles that are beginning to receive serious consideration among professional evaluators are those of evaluator as member of a profession and evaluator as member of society at large. Membership within a profession holds certain defined expectations, commonly shared by all who consider themselves part of that specific professional group. These expectations include common training, similar methods and areas of practice, and dialogue among members leading to clarification of values, education of members, and some degree of self-regulation. Frequently, evaluators are perceived as members of two professions, that of evaluation and that reflecting the discipline in which they practice. Most disciplines have limited expectations of what these dual roles should encompass, leaving the evaluator in conflict as to which profession has priority and how the two support each other.

The role of evaluator as member of society at large reflects our presence in a democratic society where common citizenship carries with it certain expectations of duty, responsibility, and practice. The functions and expectations of an evaluator in this role are not yet defined. In fact, many evaluators are not certain that this is a legitimate role of an evaluator. For others, this role is closely aligned with the concept of social justice. A major area of debate is whether evaluators examine programs, practices, people and policies within a framework of democracy and social justice, or whether it is part of the duty of evaluators to foster and ensure democracy and social justice.

The Status of Internal Evaluators. A role of the evaluator that deserves separate attention is that of internal evaluator. Professional evaluators serving in this capacity often find themselves fulfilling three sets of expectations: those related to the practice of evaluation, those related to the discipline in which they practice evaluation, and those related to the organization with which they are associated. Several reasons can be given for these conflicting expectations. Personnel reviews for internal evaluators are commonly conducted by managers or administrators with ties to the evaluators' assigned duties. Generally the reward system, including travel, paid conference attendance, continuing education, and professional benefits, reflects more clearly the discipline in which the evaluator practices and the needs of the organization than the profession of evaluation. Also, greater prominence is given to communication of study results in discipline-based journals and conferences than to those related to evaluation. A common situation that makes the internal evaluator's role even more difficult is when that role is only part time, that is, when the duties of evaluator are only part of the overall employment functions, and sometimes only temporary. In this dual role, the internal evaluator is more program or organizational staff than evaluator, and allegiance lies more with the primary role than with the evaluator role.

The conflicts of internal evaluators were voiced frequently in the development of the Guiding Principles. Many of the debates over inclusion of statements and examples focused on their interpretation in light of this role. Response to the document indicates some evaluators think the principles are not strong enough in providing support to internal evaluators, but others think the document is too strong and that internal evaluators cannot live up to the principles. Despite these difference, a common area of concern was that internal evaluators frequently perceive themselves in ethical conflict because of their duality and are uncertain as to how to resolve their conflicts. Clearly, efforts must be made to address the ethical issues faced by internal evaluators and means found to incorporate these efforts into future drafts of the Guiding Principles.

Multiculturalism and Diversity. The need to recognize and support greater understanding and knowledge of issues related to multiculturalism and diversity is part of the expanding literature of evaluation. The Guiding Principles document reflects this need in its underlying assumptions. The American Evaluation Association acknowledges that the document reflects values of the Western culture in which it was written. Members of AEA, however, are involved frequently in evaluations that are outside the bounds of Western culture. Many of our members export the practices and processes of evaluation theory and methods to cultures that have differing ethical frameworks. In these settings, within these cultures, evaluators have to address seriously the ethics of their actions and products. What is considered ethical practice in Western culture will in all probability not hold in these cultures. The same issue should be addressed in our training programs. Discussions with faculty involved in evaluator training indicate that most programs recruit and include international students. Examination of their course work, however, reveals little, if any, emphasis on recognition of different cultural requirements.

Multiculturalism and diversity are not issues of concern only to those involved in evaluation in international domains. Evaluators also encounter diversity issues and variations in cultural expectations when working at the local, regional, and national levels. Currently, little or no information is available in evaluation literature or in training programs on how evaluators can meet these needs. Rather, as professionals, we appear to have delegated diversity and cultural issues either to the "future issues" category or to have labeled them as site-specific traits. The first delegation allows us to recognize the issue but to procrastinate on doing anything about it. The second, labeling the problem as site specific, allows us to continue ignoring the problem, identifying it as one that must be our clients' concern but not ours. At a time when many of our stakeholders are actively involved in improving, clarifying, and retraining their professionals to meet the needs of diverse populations, we are still arguing over whether there is an issue.

Common Good. An underlying tenet of Western democracy is that every citizen has the responsibility to protect and defend the common good. Expectations of this role go beyond those related to social justice and encompass such topics as whistle blowing, freedom of information, and freedom of involvement. Practices called into question under the ethic of common good could include ownership of reports, fair and balanced reporting, boundaries of evaluator/client involvement, and the evaluator's right to decline involvement.

What defense of the common good means for evaluators is uncertain; however, multiple examples of ethical dilemmas related to common good can be cited. For instance, when evaluating a program, evaluators usually observe contexts outside the scope of the specified evaluation domain. If these observations indicate that undue harm is being done, what is our obligation to report the harm? And to whom? Suppose the evaluators become aware of false, limited, or non-dissemination of evaluation findings (for example, stakeholders are denied or have limited access to report findings that could provide them with the necessary data to argue with administrative decisions). What is the evaluators' duty? Do we have an obligation to report findings to stakeholders who are omitted from the decision making process? Are we obligated to inform stakeholders of negative results, or is that the prerogative of the client?

Monitoring the Practice of Evaluation. The *Guiding Principles for Evaluators* were not developed to serve as a means of monitoring the practice of evaluation. Their conception, however, reflects the growing number of ethical questions related to self-monitoring that are becoming frequent among practitioners. Metaevaluation is seen as one method of providing regulation of evaluation practice. Its use unfortunately is infrequent and even when used creates ethical questions. For instance, who should create standards of quality assurance? Evaluators? Clients? Can evaluators monitor their own work or should external evaluation be required? If metaevaluators uncover poor or inappropriate practice, to whom are they obligated to report the impropriety? The original client? The metaevaluation client? Funding agencies?

Evaluators and clients alike are seeking ways to determine the definition and structure of "good" practice. Most evaluators know too well that the reputation of our discipline and practice can be tainted by poor practice; clients have long memories and are swayed easily by past experiences. In its current state of professional development, evaluation is only at the beginning stage of self-monitoring. The establishment and support of AEA principles, Joint Committee standards (1988, 1994) and other professional guidelines specific to evaluation indicate that we are struggling with an issue that will require much introspection, more commitment, and more assessment over the next decade. It may be some time before evaluation reaches the level of professional development at which we, as peers, truly monitor our own practice in a structured and objective manner.

Role of Technology. The role of technology has had a major impact on the development of all modes of inquiry. Advances in electronic management and planning, information sharing, document storage and communication networks have changed the expectations, requests, and actions of evaluators, managers, and clients. Newer, faster, more efficient modes of collecting, analyzing, and distributing information have revolutionized the disciplines of measurement, research design, and statistical analysis. These advances, however, have also been accompanied by ethical dilemmas that should be addressed by evaluators.

For instance, the ability to produce and reproduce documents via the use of electronic transfer has made it easier for evaluators to provide tailored reports for diverse stakeholders and to address varying audience needs. We can now provide more reports, in more formats, to more people, in a more efficient and less costly manner than ever before. Use of techniques such as electronic transfer, varied multimedia presentations, and widespread distribution, however, raise ethical questions. What is the optimal amount of information? How do we ensure equity of information among multiple stakeholders? Who decides which audience receives which set of information? What is the evaluation report, the paper product, or the electronic copy and accompanying material? Who controls the release of information?

Another dilemma related to the use of technology in evaluation arises as a result of advances in sample generation, data storage, and collection of information via electronic devices. Access to huge databanks makes it easier for clients to request and evaluators to provide larger amounts of information. There is no guarantee, however, that this information will be useful to the client or will accurately portray responses to the questions under consideration. For example, in personnel evaluation, is it really necessary to obtain the work load, including specific tasks, of all staff and their accompanying salaries to determine if equity raises are merited? Although the computer with spreadsheets will handle a seemingly infinite number of demographic variables, should nonessential information be collected as a baseline for possible future studies? When does over-collection and massive storage of information infringe on the rights of respondents and become a threat to confidentiality? In other words, how do evaluators and clients decide that "enough is enough"?

Other questions related to advances in the ability to store and retrieve large amounts of information include ownership of information, how long data should be stored, who should have access to the information, and security of files. Although these issues were present in varying degree prior to technological advances, the rapid ability to access, share, re-examine and reproduce information has made them more serious and more frequent. Currently, many users of evaluation are struggling with these issues, attempting to find solutions to what they perceive already to be an ethical issue. Evaluators, however, have not yet begun a concentrated dialogue on ethical uses of advanced technology in a way that reflects our unique viewpoint, and we are lagging behind our clients when these practices are questioned.

Definition of Evaluation. An important issue pertaining to the future development of an ethic of evaluation is that related to the definition of evaluation. In the development of the *Guiding Principles for Evaluators*, it became apparent that multiple meanings are ascribed to the term "evaluation," each representing different practices, disciplines, and entities. Although the majority of AEA members practice program evaluation, one of the underlying assumptions made in the development of the document was that the Guiding Principles would encompass all aspects of evaluation, including program, product, personnel, curriculum, and policy studies. The principles also were to reflect evaluation as practiced in multiple disciplines and settings. Additional efforts were made to ensure that no philosophy or methodological bias related to the qualitative/quantitative debate was reflected in the document. Instead, the principles are intended to transcend these subcomponents of evaluation, encompassing the entire entity.

The consequence of this enlarged, encompassing perception of evaluation was that no inclusive definition of evaluation or evaluator was available. Assumptions A and B allude to a tentative statement of what evaluation is; however, no definition of evaluation was stated in the document. It was easier to determine what evaluation was not (statistics, research, measurement, planning, affirmative action, program administration) than it was to determine what evaluation is.

In his review of the Guiding Principles, Rossi comments on this missing component. This is a valid criticism, and one that should be addressed by the AEA membership. Several questions pertain to this issue. Is evaluation more than providing information to decision makers? Is it more than valuing and making judgments? Are we obligated to search for, find, and report the truth? Is there a truth to be found? If so, this has a tremendous impact on how we judge our own, other evaluators', and clients' actions. The current movement toward the delineation of theories and philosophies of evaluation will aid in this discussion. Development of these theories and philosophies must include the status of ethics when defining and exemplifying evaluation. If divergent perceptions of ethical practice occur based on the development of alternate definitions of evaluation, the utility of the Guiding Principles must be reexamined. If differing contextual settings (for example, personnel, product, program, or curriculum evaluation) develop to the point of supporting different ethical systems, then alternate guidelines may have to be developed, reflecting a broader, encompassing definition of evaluation.

Client Status in Evaluation Ethics. Development of the Guiding Principles focused on what is ethical practice for evaluators. The document reflects what is currently considered, or is hoped to be considered, appropriate actions for those who call themselves evaluators. Evaluation, however, is a communication, a dialogue, among evaluators and clients, with emphasis on sharing information. An underdeveloped area of evaluation ethics is that pertaining to the clients whom we serve. The principles should be seen as an ethical system not only for evaluators but also for those whom evaluators serve.

A more complete ethical model of evaluation should provide evaluators with principles guiding their process and practice; inform clients of evaluators' obligations and duties; provide clients with principles guiding their involvement in the process and practice of evaluation; inform evaluators of clients' obligations and duties. This multidimensional aspect of the Guiding Principles is not yet complete. Current discussions on evaluation ethics tend to focus on the first point, developing ethical guidelines for evaluators. As part of this development, there has been some, albeit limited discussion on the second point, informing clients of what is ethical evaluation practice on the part of the evaluator. As Chelimsky points out in her response to the Guiding Principles, this approach leads to the impression that ethical evaluation is the sole responsibility of evaluators, without acknowledging the clients' obligations. The current emphasis on parts one and two reduces evaluation from a model of communication and dialogue between two or more entities to a unidimensional, one-way model. The future development of this aspect of the principles and its use by evaluators and clients will greatly influence the future of evaluation theory and practice. As evaluators and clients together establish boundaries for the ethic of their interaction, the face of evaluation will change. If this aspect of ethical evaluation is delayed in its development or ignored, further progress toward the growth of evaluation as a profession also will be delayed.

Additional Issues for Future Development. Other issues will impact the future development of ethics in evaluation and should be addressed. These include the relationship of the Guiding Principles to other documents addressing ethical practice in evaluation, such as the Joint Committee standards (1988,

1994); the relationship of this document and its use in practice to principles and ethical standards for disciplines in which evaluation is practiced (for example, American Psychological Association, American Educational Research Association, General Accounting Office standards); the relationship of the principles to ethical theories in general. Ethical issues pertaining to the role of funding sources in monitoring evaluation and evaluator accountability to these sources should be explored. Ethical dialogues between clients, consumers, and evaluators should include topics such as confidentiality of sources, management of information, and ownership of reports. The changing face of evaluation, especially as it encompasses participatory evaluation, empowerment, and shared decision making also will have implications for the ethics of future practice.

Working Through the Agenda: Continuing the Dialogue

Given this agenda of issues pertaining to the ethics of evaluation, we must now ask how we can begin to address the items. To aid in that process, I offer the following suggestions.

Education and Socialization. Two major methods of integrating the concept of ethical practice in the discipline of evaluation make use of education and socialization practices. Education involves use of structured approaches to teaching and discussing the concepts of ethics; socialization involves indirect methods of integration such that their use and functions become a common component of the society of those who are evaluators.

Education. The status of education in ethical practice within the discipline of evaluation is limited. Although most of the current texts on evaluation contain limited sections on the topic (Posavac and Cary, 1992; Rossi and Freeman, 1993; Shadish, Cook, and Leviton, 1991; Worthen and Sanders, 1987), no structure is established, either formally or informally, for training evaluators or clients on ethical practice. As evaluation ethics advance and solidify in the future, several such structures could and should be developed. These include pre-service, in-service, and transdisciplinary education.

Pre-Service Education. Pre-service education encompasses the training of future evaluators. A recent training directory (Altschuld and Engle, 1994) identifies forty-nine programs specializing in the training of evaluators. Examination of the curriculum provided across these programs gives no indication that ethics or the practice of ethical behavior is a major component of any of the curricula. This absence of formal training is very noticeable when compared to the curriculum of professionals representing the fields in which evaluation plays a major role, such as mental health, public health, educational administration, business, and criminal justice. Formal training in these disciplines usually requires a separate course on ethical practice. Evaluators who receive their primary training within these discipline contexts may have a solid background in the ethics of their discipline but generally will have had no introduction to standards or literature pertaining to ethics in evaluation.

Curricular materials encompassing ethics should be developed immediately. This could include increasing the coverage of ethics in current texts, developing texts for the sole purpose of addressing evaluation ethics, and creating a casebook of ethical dilemmas in evaluation. These variations could be integrated into pre-existing pre-service courses in evaluation to expand coverage of ethical issues. Teachers of evaluation should work with each other to establish standards for what constitutes appropriate coverage of ethics in the training of evaluators. Initially this work could be an informal sharing of information that over time could be used to establish quality control of content. These actions could be sponsored by such groups as the Topical Interest Group: Teaching of Evaluation, a component of AEA. As the profession advances and establishes a more formal training curriculum, the inclusion of ethics as part of a core curriculum and the extent of that inclusion should be addressed.

In-Service Education. In-service education typically encompasses continued education for professionals who are already in the field. The audience for this format of educational service includes those who are now employed as professional evaluators, either on a part-time or full-time basis, as well as those who will become involved as evaluators in the future, either through direct training or work requirements. In-service training in ethical practice could involve the development of formal, structured materials that could be used by professionals who are already experiencing the ethical dilemmas of evaluation. Materials could include self-study packets, workshops, special courses, and association-sponsored continuing education units. Whereas some organizations may be large enough to sponsor their own workshops, AEA may wish to include this as part of its annual meeting workshop sequence, or regional workshops could be held on a periodic basis. Regional evaluation organizations could be involved in this type of education, providing time and place for evaluators to gather to study specific issues related to ethics.

Socialization. Socialization includes the integration and assimilation of information, material, and people within an organized body. As indicated in the introduction to the Guiding Principles, the purpose of the document is not to monitor evaluators but to aid in the socialization of a sense of ethics within our larger peer group. We can aid this process in multiple ways. The American Evaluation Association and its affiliated regional organizations can allot time and people to this process. Presentations related to current research theory and practice as it reflects ethical issues can be encouraged. Periodic annual conferences can be dedicated to the topic of ethical practice. Open sessions pertaining to the discussion of ethical conflicts can be established. Ethics committees can be established and become active in presenting, reviewing, and discussing ethical dilemmas that evaluators or clients are currently experiencing.

Continued Development of Written Ethical Systems. The development of a written set of ethical standards is considered a mark of professional maturation. With the development of the Guiding Principles, evaluation has a preliminary document that can provide some assistance to evaluators when making ethical decisions. The process of creating a written document, however, must not stop at this point. Several things must occur in the development of the written documentation of our ethical system. First, as noted in the document (Assumption J), the Guiding Principles are not considered to be in their final form but should be reviewed, revised, and expanded on a continual basis to guide and reflect the growth of the profession. The inclusion of a sunset provision was deemed important in maintaining the viability of the document. Formal periodic review of this document, as a reflection of the status of evaluation, is necessary. Development of the initial document reflects the current thinking of the majority of evaluators; it does not include perceptions of evaluation clients, consumers, or other stakeholders. Future reviews should include representatives of these groups.

The second development that should occur in the evolution of written documentation of our ethical system is comparison of the Guiding Principles with written standards for evaluation. The purpose of the principles was to provide a set of commonly shared beliefs about the ethical practice of evaluation. This differs from standards, which provide rules or direct guidelines, each of which are considered appropriate in their own right and are more explicit in terms of what is considered correct practice. The most well-known and most frequently used evaluation standards are those produced by the Joint Committee (1988, 1994). Although developed for use in educational settings, the standards have been shown to be appropriate in health, mental health, and social service settings. Sections of other written standards, such as those developed by the American Educational Research Association, the National Council on Measurement in Education, and the American Psychological Association, should be reviewed to determine if the Guiding Principles overlay the standards supported by their membership.

Third, at some point in the future, evaluators will have to address the need to develop our own set of standards and the role that these standards will have in focusing the membership in our profession. Although as a profession we have not yet matured to the point of monitoring our ethical practice, nor of delineating specific rules of acceptable practice, the time will come when we must consider if we are mature enough to reach this common agreement. If so, written documentation that encompasses many of the preliminary topics found in the current Guiding Principles and in the multiple sets of standards used by evaluators will have to be developed and documented.

Research on Ethical Practice. A concurrent method of examining agenda items is through the lens of a researcher. As the ethic of evaluation matures via the development of theories, educational materials, and written documentation of dialogues, it is natural that research focusing on the relationship of ethics and evaluation will be developed to a greater degree. At the current time, several studies have investigated the status of evaluation ethics. Honea (1991) and Morris and Cohn (1993) obtained practicing evaluators' perceptions of ethical practice; Toms (1993) examined differences in evaluation ethics among

Canadian and U.S. evaluators; Newman, Brown (Newman and Brown, 1992; Brown and Newman, 1992) have posited and tested a theoretical framework for making ethical decisions pertaining to evaluation. Work similar to these studies should be encouraged and expanded. The questions posed by each agenda issue could be examined via research methods that would enhance the dialogue on ethics in evaluation. In particular, research should be conducted that focuses on the utility of the Guiding Principles, the ability of clients and consumers to use them, evaluators' perceptions of their strengths and weaknesses, and how the principles could better reflect the theories and practice of evaluation.

The development of this research is not an easy task. The methodologies, contextual settings, and respondents are numerous and, if properly examined, would include the life work of many researchers. The richness of this research in terms of both its utility and its theory, however, make the field one that should be considered a priority among those interested in the discipline of evaluation.

Role of the Stakeholder. A last means of approaching the agenda that deserves special notation is one alluded to throughout much of the above—the role of the stakeholder in the practice of ethical evaluation. Evaluation is considered a service profession; we conduct evaluations for others to use; our judgments are to aid others in their decision-making process. Currently much of evaluation literature on ethics focuses on the development, growth, and monitoring of the evaluator's system of ethics. This focus should shift to a system of ethics that encompasses the role of the client in the development of evaluation ethics. We now must begin to put equal emphasis on training the client how ethically to propose and commission an evaluation, how ethically to interact during an evaluation, and how ethically to use evaluation information.

The process of client-focused education and socialization is more difficult to conceptualize and maintain than is the process for evaluators. We have a direct interest in improving our knowledge base and practice of evaluation and can perceive direct consequences of ethical practice. These direct consequences are not as readily apparent to our clients and stakeholders. This is not surprising; as stakeholders in non-evaluation transactions, we lack similar knowledge and motivation. We expect our doctor and our accountant to be ethical when working with us, but in general we are not aware of our ethical responsibility when working with them. Just as we struggle to balance our consumer rights and responsibilities, so do our stakeholders struggle to balance their rights and responsibilities. It is part of our function to help educate them in this role.

Starting on the Path

The *Guiding Principles for Evaluators* provides the profession of evaluation with a beginning point for ethical development. Though not complete, and not comprehensive, the document gives us the starting point for a dialogue that should continue over several decades. The document does not provide right answers or give us a standard way of conducting our practice; it does provide us with guidelines that will aid our thinking and help us when having to make ethical decisions. Users of the document will find many ways that the document could and should be improved. These findings should not be used to discredit the document but should be shared with the organization in our search for a common ethical system.

In its current state, the status of ethics in evaluation is at an early stage of development. We know we need ethics to survive; we know we, not others, must develop our ethical system; we know that we must not put off this task. We have begun the discussion; we have developed a preliminary document. We must not let the process stop at this point; we must continue the dialogue and where necessary create and recreate our own path to ethical practice.

References

Altschuld, J. W., and Engle, M. (eds.). *The Preparation of Professional Evaluators: Issues, Perspectives, and Programs.* New Directions for Program Evaluation, no. 62. San Francisco: Jossey-Bass, 1994.

Brown, R. D., and Newman, D. L. "Ethical Principles and Evaluation Standards: Do They Match?" *Evaluation Review*, 1992, *16* (6), 650–663.

Honea, G. "Ethical Dilemmas in Evaluation: Interviews of Evaluators." Paper presented at the annual meeting of the American Evaluation Association, Washington, D.C., Nov., 1991.

Joint Committee on Standards for Educational Evaluation. *Personnel Evaluation Standards.* Newbury Park, Calif.: Sage, 1988.

Joint Committee on Standards for Educational Evaluation. *Program Evaluation Standards.* Newbury Park, Calif.: Sage, 1994.

Morris, M., and Cohn, R. "Program Evaluators and Ethical Challenges: A National Survey." *Evaluation Review*, 1993, *17* (6) 621–642.

Newman, D.L., and Brown, R.D., "Violations of Evaluation Standards: Frequency and Seriousness of Occurrence." *Evaluation Review*, 1992, *16* (3), 219–234.

Posavac, E. J., and Carey, R. J. *Program Evaluation: Method and Case Study.* (4th ed.) Englewood Cliffs, N.J.: Prentice-Hall, 1992.

Rossi, P.H., and Freeman, H.E. *Evaluation: A Systematic Approach.* (5th ed.) Newbury Park, Calif.: Sage, 1993.

Shadish, W. R., Cook, T. D., and Leviton, L. C. *Foundations of Program Evaluation: Theories of Practice.* Newbury Park, Calif.: Sage, 1991.

Toms, K. "A Canadian-American Cross National Study of the Personal and Professional Ethics of Evaluators." Unpublished dissertation, University at Albany/SUNY, 1993.

Worthen, B. R., and Sanders, J.R. *Educational Evaluation.* White Plains, N.Y.: Longman, 1987.

DIANNA L. NEWMAN *is associate professor specializing in program evaluation, School of Education, University at Albany/SUNY, and director of the Evaluation Consortium at Albany.*

INDEX

Africa, evaluation in, 82
Aid to Families with Dependent Children (AFDC), 63
Altschuld, J. W., 106
American Anthropological Association, 5
American Educational Research Association (AERA), 5, 16, 47-48
American Evaluation Association (AEA), 3, 19, 35, 47, 77. *See also* Guiding principles, American Evaluation Association
American Psychological Association (APA), 5, 47-48
American Society for Public Administration (ASPA), 64
Austin, D., 3
Australasia, evaluation in, 81, 85

Babcock, J., 15
Barnes, C., 95, 96
Belmont Report, 5
Bemelmans-Videc, M., commentary by, 78, 80, 84, 86
Beno et al. v. Shalala, 66
Brewer, R. M., 93
Brown, R. D., 6, 109

Campbell, D. T., 77
Canada, evaluation in, 85
Care, N., 29
Carey, R. G., 77
Carey, R. J., 106
Chandler, R. D., 64
Clientism, 29
Clients: and ethics of evaluation, 105; and evaluators, 25-26, 29; and guiding principles, 29, 87. *See also* Stakeholders
Codes of ethics. *See* Ethics: codes of
Cohn, R., 109
Common good. *See* Public interest
Comptroller General, 5
Conner, R. F., 30, 78
Contractualism, 29
Cook, J. A., 95
Cook, T. D., 5, 77, 106
Cooley, L. S., commentary by, 79-80, 84, 86, 88
Covert, R. W., 44

Danziger, S., 65
Denmark, evaluation in, 86
Diversity: and cultural variance, 93; and ethics, 101-102; and evaluators, 25, 93; and feminism, 92; and guiding principles, 20-21, 25, 32. *See also* Feminists; Minorities; Multiculturalism; Persons with disabilities
Dougherty, K., 32
Duncan, R., commentary by, 79, 84-85

Education: and evaluation, 106-107; in-service, 107; preservice, 106-107
Empowerment, 91
Engle, M., 106
ERS Standards. *See* Standards for Program Evaluation, Evaluation Research Society
Ethical Principles of Psychologists and Code of Conduct, American Psychological Association, 5, 47
Ethical Standards of the American Educational Research Association, 5, 47
Ethics: addressing issues of, in evaluation, 106-110; and client status, 105; codes of, 55-56; and common good, 102; and defining evaluation, 104-105; difficulty of, discussion, 27-28; and diversity, 101-102; domains of, 44; and education, 106-107; of evaluation studies, 28; evaluators', problems, 29-30; and evaluators' roles/expectations, 99-101; and internal evaluators, 101; issues of, in evaluation, 99-106; of language use, 95; of marginalized people, 92; and monitoring evaluation, 102-103; and multiculturalism, 101-102; and practice, 108-109; and professional conflict, 28; and socialization, 107; and stakeholders, 109; and technology, 103-104; and value-free tradition, 27, 31; written documents of, 107-108. *See also* Guiding principles, American Evaluation Association; Standards; Values
Evaluation: addressing ethical issues in, 106-110; in Africa, 82; in Australasia, 81, 85; in Canada, 85; and clientism, 29; and clients, 29, 87, 105; and contractualism, 29; and data collection decisions,

Evaluation (*continued*)
94-95; defining, 15, 104-105; in Denmark, 86; and education, 106-107; emancipatory framework for, 92-93, 95-96; and empowerment, 91; ethical fallacies of, 28-30; ethical issues in, 99-106; and freedom of information, 14; and good practice, 103; hybrid model of, 9; important attributes of, 37; in India, 81, 83, 87; and marginalized people, 92-93; and methodologicalism, 29-30; monitoring, 102-103; multifacted/diverse nature of, 20, 83; negative effects of, 24; participatory models of, 93; and pluralism/elitism, 30; principles appropriate for, 6-8; and program theory, 94; professionalization of, 6, 21, 108; and public interest, 10-14, 32-33; purposes of, 20-21; and relativism, 30; reporting, findings, 95; requests for, 61-63; research on ethical, 108-109; and social equity, 24-25; and social justice, 91; and socialization, 107; and stakeholders, 109; and technology, 103-104; and telecommunications, 74; and welfare reform, 65-66. *See also* Guiding principles, American Evaluation Association; Program evaluation

Evaluation Network (ENet), 3, 19

Evaluation Research Society, program evaluation standards of, 19

Evaluation Research Society Standards Committee, 3, 5, 28

Evaluation Resources, Inc. (ERI), 69-70

Evaluators: approaches of, 22; attacks on, 53; and autonomy, 9-10; client responsibilities of, 29; and client vs. other needs, 25-26; communication of, 22, 25; competence of, 22-23; and contracts, 29; and confidentiality, 73; continuing education of, 23; courage of, 53, 58; and diversity, 25, 93, 102; education of, 22; educational 28; ethical problems of, 28-30; and evaluation studies, 94; expectations of, 100; and financial disclosure, 24; and freedom of information, 14, 25; and funding agencies, 84; and harmful evaluative results, 24; integrity/honesty of, 23-24; and methodology, 29-30; and multiculturalism, 25, 30, 83; and new approaches, 72; and particular professional standards, 24; and pluralism/elitism, 30; and political action, 95-96; and power relationships, 94; professional limits of, 22; and public interest, 10-14, 25-26, 32-33, 102; and relativism, 30; and respondents' needs/rights, 85; and respect for people, 24-25; responsibilties of, 96; roles of, 96, 99-101; self-monitoring of, 103; and social equity, 24-25; and speaking truth, 54, 58; and stakeholder interests, 25; subservient role of, 10; systematic inquiry by, 22; and technical standards, 22; and validity/reliability, 91-92. *See also* Guiding principles, American Evaluation Association; Internal evaluators

Farley, J., 93, 96
Feminists: criticisms of, 93; and diversity, 92; and emancipatory framework, 92, 96; and evaluation studies/findings, 92, 95
Fonow, M. M., 95
Foster, S., 95, 96
Freeman, H. E., 77, 106

GAO Standards. *See Government Auditing Standards*, U.S. General Accounting Office
Ginsberg, P., commentary by, 79, 84-85
Glassner, B., 3
Government Auditing Standards, U.S. General Accounting Office, 5, 37-42
Guba, E. G., 15
Guiding principles, American Evaluation Association: assumptions underlying, 20-22, 70-71, 77; and autonomy, 9-10; background of, 3-5, 19, 47; and clients, 29, 87, 105; and competence, 22-23, 43, 56-57, 72, 83-84; compromised nature of, 16; and criteria for use, 70-71; critique of, 31-33, 53-59; debate over, 3-4; and decisional independence, 9; and definition of evaluation, 15, 104-105; development of, 5-16; disagreement about, 7; disclaimer of, 16; document of, 19-26; early drafts of, 6-15; and ethical fallacies, 31-32; and ethical issues, 99-110; and evaluators' needs, 54; and evaluators' speaking truth to power, 54; feedback on, 15-16; final draft of, 15-16; and freedom, 85; and freedom of information, 14; generality of, 59; graduate student reaction to, 42-44; human rights concerns of, 40; and hybrid evaluation model, 9; and inclu-

siveness, 40; and independent consultants, 69-74; and informed consent, 66; and inter-/intraorganizational politics, 8; and internal evaluators, 61-67, 101; and integrity/honesty, 23-24, 31, 43-44, 57, 72-73, 84; international perspectives on, 77-90; and Joint Committee Program Evaluation Standards, 48-52; language of, 14-15, 40-41, 59; legal ramifications of, 16; major issues of, 7-15; as means, 15; and methodology, 31, 40; and misuse correction, 62-65; and multiculturalism/diversity, 21-22, 25, 32, 44, 58, 71, 101-102; and other standards documents, 3, 5, 19, 21, 37-42, 106, 108; and other obligations, 12-14; overall applicability of, 90-82; periodic review of, 22; and pluralism/elitism, 33; and professionalization of evaluation, 6, 44, 81, 108; and program evaluation, 8; and public interest/welfare, 10-14, 25-26, 32-33, 41-42, 57, 73-74, 85-87; and qualitative-quantitative dispute, 31; questions regarding, 49, 52; real-life testing of, 70; reasons for, 3-4; recommendations for use of, 44-45; and relativism vs. cultural relativism, 31-32; and respect for people, 24-25, 31-32, 41, 44, 73, 84-85, 91; and review body, 58-59; sequence of events for, 5-7, 16; and stakeholders' interests, 63, 72-73; vs. standards, 4-5; and standards of practice, 48, 71; and systematic inquiry, 22, 31, 43, 71, 82-83; task force activities, 4-16, 19-20; task force members, 5-6; task force results, 4; and third world, 87; and Topical Interest Groups, 70-71, 107; and types of evaluation, 7-9; usefulness of, 70; as weak, 56; and work-setting limitations, 15; and yardsticks for practice, 16

Halberstam, D., 27
Harding, S., 92
Hendricks, M., 78
Hjelholt, G., commentary by, 79, 81-82, 86-87
Hornea, F., 109
Hornea, G. E., 44
House, E. R., 29, 32
Howe, K., 32

India, evaluation in, 81, 83, 87

Informed consent, 65-66
Internal evaluators: and colleague pressures, 63; and conflict of interest, 62, 84; and conflict resolution, 62; conflicts of, 101; constraints of, 15; ethical considerations of, 62-66; and evaluation requests, 61-63; expectations of, 101; and informed consent, 65-66; and management relations, 62; and misuse correction, 63-65; and negative evaluations, 62; reputation of, 63; and stakeholders' interests, 63; status of, 101; and time limitations, 62, 74. *See also* Evaluators

Joint Committee on Standards for Educational Evaluation, 3, 5, 28, 37, 47, 48, 103, 106, 108
Joint Committee Standards. *See Program Evaluation Standards*, Joint Committee on Standards for Educational Evaluation; *Standards for Evaluations of Education Programs, Projects, and Materials*, Joint Committee on Standards for Educational Evaluation

Kossoudji, S., 65

Lather, P., 92
Leviton, L. C., 5, 106
Lincoln, Y. S., 15
Love, A. J., commentary by, 79-83, 85, 88
Lovell, R., 65

McLaughlin, J., 92
Madison, A. M., 92, 93, 96
Martin, J., 95
Mertens, D. M., 92, 93, 96
Metaevaluation, 103
Methodologicalism, 29-30
Minorities: and emancipatory framework, 92, 96; and evaluation findings, 95; and evaluation studies, 92; and power, 93-94
Morris, M., 109
Multiculturalism: and ethics, 101-102; and evaluation research, 92-95; and evaluators, 25, 30, 83; and guiding principles, 21-22, 25, 32, 44, 58, 71. *See also* Diversity; Minorities

National Commission for the Protection of Human Subjects of Biomedical and Behavioral Research, 5

National Council on Measurement in Education (NCME), 47-48
Newman, D. L., 6, 109
Nigro, L. G., 64

Oliver, M., 92, 94, 96

Patton, M. W., 77
Persons with disabilities: and emancipatory framework, 92, 95-96; and evaluation findings, 95; and evaluation studies, 92-93; positivist vs. emancipatory studies on, 94-95; recognizing, 93
Pluralism/elitism, 30
Pollard, D. S., 93
Posavac, E. J., 77, 106
Power: and emancipatory framework, 93-94; inequities of, 93-95; speaking truth to, 54
Program evaluation: demand for, 61; and guiding principles, 8; and in-house evaluation units, 61; and program theory, 94; standards for, 3, 8, 19. *See also* Evaluation
Program Evaluation Standards, Joint Committee on Standards for Educational Evaluation, 3, 47-52
Protection of Human Subjects, 5
Public good. *See* Public interest
Public interest: defining, 33; diversity of, 32-33; and ethics, 102; and evaluators, 10-14, 25-26, 32-33, 102; and freedom, 32; and freedom of information, 14; and guiding principles, 10-14, 32-33; and individual/group interests, 33; and social justice, 32; and telecommunications, 74

Reed, L. R., 65
Reinharz, S., 92
Relativism, 30
Richardson, W. D., 64
Ross, D., 27
Rossi, P. H., 4, 37, 77, 106
Rugh, J., commentary by, 79, 84-85
Rwampororo, R., commentary by, 79, 82, 84

Sanders, J. R., 48, 106
Scriven, M., 49, 63
Sechrest, L., 15
Shadish, W. R., 5, 106
Sharp, C. A., commentary by, 79, 81-82, 88

Sieber, J. E., 28, 30
Singh, A. K., commentary by, 79-81, 83-84, 87
Singleton, P., 93, 95, 96
Sinha, J. B., commentary by, 80-81, 83-84, 87
Smith, B., 15
Social justice: and evaluation, 91; and public interest, 32
Speaking truth to power, 54
Stakeholders: and ethical evaluation, 109; and guiding principles, 72-73; and internal evaluators, 63. *See also* Clients
Standards: American Society for Public Administrators, 64; description of, 55-56; Evaluation Research Society, 3; and good practice, 103; Joint Committee for Educational Evaluation, 3; particular professional, 24; for program evaluation, 3, 8, 19; and professionalization, 108; proliferation of, 49, 52. *See also* Ethics; *Government Auditing Standards*, U.S. General Accounting Office; Guiding principles, American Evaluation Association; *Program Evaluation Standards*, Joint Committee on Standards for Educational Evaluation; *Standards for Evaluations of Education Programs, Projects, and Materials*, Joint Committee on Standards for Educational Evaluation; *Standards for Program Evaluation*, Evaluation Research Society; Values
Standards for Evaluations of Education Programs, Projects, and Materials, Joint Committee on Standards for Educational Evaluation, 3, 5, 37-42, 47
Standards for Program Evaluation, Evaluation Research Society, 3, 5, 37-42
Stanfield, J. H., 91, 95
Steady, F. C., 92, 96
Stufflebeam, D. L., 28, 52

Technology: and evaluation, 103-104; and public interest, 74
Telecommunications, 74
Terry, R., 93
Toms, K., 109
Truth: and evaluator's role, 58; speaking, to power, 54

U.S. Department of Health and Human Services (DHHS), 65

U.S. General Accounting Office, 37

Value-free tradition, 27, 31
Values: and Cold War environment, 27-28; difficulty of, discussion, 27-28; and professional conflict, 28; and social science, 27; and value-free tradition, 27, 31. *See also* Ethics; Guiding principles, American Evaluation Association; Standards
Villegas, A. M., 94

Welfare: and American underclass, 66; and informed consent, 65-66; and Michigan waiver study, 65-66; and stakeholders' interests, 63
White, A., 95
Winston, J., commentary by, 80-81
Wiseman, M. 66
Worthen, B. R., 106

Zarb, G., 93

Ordering Information

NEW DIRECTIONS FOR PROGRAM EVALUATION is a series of paperback books that presents the latest techniques and procedures for conducting useful evaluation studies of all types of programs. Books in the series are published quarterly in Spring, Summer, Fall, and Winter and are available for purchase by subscription as well as by single copy.

SUBSCRIPTIONS for 1995 cost $56.00 for individuals (a savings of 22 percent over single-copy prices) and $78.00 for institutions, agencies, and libraries. Please do not send institutional checks for personal subscriptions. Standing orders are accepted.

SINGLE COPIES cost $17.95 when payment accompanies order. (California, New Jersey, New York, and Washington, D.C., residents please include appropriate sales tax.) Billed orders will be charged postage and handling.

DISCOUNTS FOR QUANTITY ORDERS are available. Please write to the address below for information.

ALL ORDERS must include either the name of an individual or an official purchase order number. Please submit your order as follows:
   Subscriptions: specify series and year subscription is to begin
   Single copies: include individual title code (such as PE59)

MAIL ALL ORDERS TO:
   Jossey-Bass Publishers
   350 Sansome Street
   San Francisco, California 94104-1342

FOR SUBSCRIPTION SALES OUTSIDE OF THE UNITED STATES, CONTACT:
   any international subscription agency or Jossey-Bass directly.

OTHER TITLES AVAILABLE IN THE
NEW DIRECTIONS FOR PROGRAM EVALUATION SERIES
William R. Shadish, Editor-in-Chief

PE65	Emerging Roles of Evaluation in Science Education Reform, *Rita G. O'Sullivan*
PE64	Preventing the Misuse of Evaluation, *Carla J. Stevens, Micah Dial*
PE63	Critically Evaluating the Role of Experiments, *Kendon J. Conrad*
PE62	The Preparation of Professional Evaluators: Issues, Perspectives, and Programs, *James W. Altschuld, Molly Engle*
PE61	The Qualitative-Quantitative Debate: New Perspectives, *Charles S. Reichardt, Sharon E. Rallis*
PE60	Program Evaluation: A Pluralistic Enterprise, *Lee Sechrest*
PE59	Evaluating Chicago School Reform, *Richard P. Niemiec, Herbert J. Walberg*
PE58	Hard-Won Lessons in Program Evaluation, *Michael Scriven*
PE57	Understanding Causes and Generalizing About Them, *Lee B. Sechrest, Anne G. Scott*
PE56	Varieties of Investigative Evaluation, *Nick L. Smith*
PE55	Evaluation in the Federal Government: Changes, Trends, and Opportunities, *Christopher G. Wye, Richard C. Sonnichsen*
PE54	Evaluating Mental Health Services for Children, *Leonard Bickman, Debra J. Rog*
PE53	Minority Issues in Program Evaluation, *Anna-Marie Madison*
PE52	Evaluating Programs for the Homeless, *Debra J. Rog*
PE51	Evaluation and Privatization: Cases in Waste Management, *John G. Heilman*
PE50	Multisite Evaluations, *Robin S. Turpin, James M. Sinacore*
PE49	Organizations in Transition: Opportunities and Challenges for Evaluation, *Colleen L. Larson, Hallie Preskill*
PE48	Inspectors General: A New Force in Evaluation, *Michael Hendricks, Michael F. Mangano, Wiliam C. Moran*
PE47	Advances in Program Theory, *Leonard Bickman*
PE46	Evaluating AIDS Prevention: Contributions of Multiple Disciplines, *Laura C. Leviton, Andrea M. Hegedus, Alan Kubrin*
PE45	Evaluation and Social Justice: Issues in Public Education, *Kenneth A. Sirotnik*
PE44	Evaluating Training Programs in Business and Industry, *Robert O. Brinkerhoff*
PE43	Evaluating Health Promotion Programs, *Marc T. Braverman*
PE41	Evaluation and the Federal Decision Maker, *Gerald L. Barkdoll, James B. Bell*
PE40	Evaluating Program Environments, *Kendon J. Conrad, Cynthia Roberts-Gray*
PE39	Evaluation Utilization, *John A. McLaughlin, Larry J. Weber, Robert W. Covert, Robert B. Ingle*
PE38	Timely, Lost-Cost Evaluation in the Public Sector, *Christopher G. Wye, Harry P. Hatry*
PE36	The Client Perspective on Evaluation, *Jeri Nowakowski*
PE35	Multiple Methods in Program Evaluation, *Melvin M. Mark, R. Lance Shotland*
PE33	Using Program Theory in Evaluation, *Leonard Bickman*
PE31	Advances in Quasi-Experimental Design and Analysis, *William M. K. Trochim*
PE30	Naturalistic Evaluation, *David D. Williams*